D1116962

TRANSLATION
AN ELIZABETHAN ART

LONDON : HUMPHREY MILFORD

OXFORD UNIVERSITY PRESS

TRANSLATION

AN ELIZABETHAN ART

BY

F. O. MATTHIESSEN

HARVARD UNIVERSITY PRESS

CAMBRIDGE, MASSACHUSETTS

1931

PRINTED AT THE HARVARD UNIVERSITY PRESS

CAMBRIDGE, MASS., U. S. A.

TO

ROBERT DUDLEY FRENCH

Prefatory Note

THE idea for this book was suggested by the late Charles Whibley's penetrating analysis of the importance of the Elizabethan translations, in *The Cambridge History of English Literature* (Volume IV, Chapter I), a suggestion that was given further stimulus by the excellent introductions to various volumes in the Tudor Translations. Three of these, by Sir Walter Raleigh to Hoby's *Courtier*, 1561 (London, 1900), by George Wyndham to North's *Plutarch*, 1579 (London, 1895), and by Charles Whibley to Holland's *Suetonius*, 1606 (London, 1899), have been invaluable. Especially good among the others are: that by W. P. Ker to Berners' *Froissart*, 1523–25 (London, 1901), to illustrate a translation made a generation before Elizabeth's reign; those by Charles Whibley to Richard Adlington's *Apuleius*, 1566 (London, 1893), and to Thomas Underdowne's *Heliodorus*, c. 1569 (London, 1895); that by James Fitzmaurice-Kelly to Shelton's *Don Quixote*, 1612, 1620 (London, 1896); and that by Charles Whibley to Urquhart and Motteux's *Rabelais*, 1653 and 1694 (London, 1900), to illustrate a very great translation later than my period. It would be hard to exaggerate my obligations to this group of recent scholars,

and especially to Charles Whibley, who, with W. E.
Henley, was chiefly responsible for the splendid revival
of Elizabethan prose in the Tudor Translations series,
and to whose critical genius so many of its introductions
stand as a monument.

In the chapters on Florio and Holland my labors
were considerably shortened by two German theses:
F. Dieckow, *John Florio's Englische Ube. .zung der
Essais Montaigne's* (Strassburg, 1903); and A. Schäfer,
Die volkstümliche Liviusübersetzung Philemon Holland's
(Burgstädt, 1910).

Among my more immediate debts I owe most to the
kindly interest and fertile suggestions of Professor John
L. Lowes, under whose direction this book was first
begun as a doctoral thesis; and to the extremely helpful
criticism of Professor George L. Kittredge and Professor
Hyder E. Rollins. I am also grateful to a number of
friends for reading the manuscript in its various stages,
and to Miss Eleonore Pollak-Ottendorf for her un-
flagging attention to the proofs.

CAMBRIDGE, MASSACHUSETTS
    JANUARY, 1931

Contents

TRANSLATION
AN ELIZABETHAN ART

CHAPTER I

Introduction

A STUDY of Elizabethan translations is a study of the means by which the Renaissance came to England. The nation had grown conscious of its cultural inferiority to the Continent, and suddenly burned with the desire to excel its rivals in letters, as well as in ships and gold. The translator's work was an act of patriotism. He, too, as well as the voyager and merchant, could do some good for his country: he believed that foreign books were just as important for England's destiny as the discoveries of her seamen, and he brought them into his native speech with all the enthusiasm of a conquest. And when you set his result beside the original, you find out a great deal about the Elizabethan mind. For you perceive what learning meant to him, and why he was so fired with enthusiasm to attain it; what is more significant, you understand the forces which actuated the development of the language in the sixteenth century, the qualities its writers strove to express, the difficulties they had to compass, and the ends they achieved.

An important thing to remember from the outset is that the Elizabethan translator did not write for the learned alone, but for the whole country. He possessed

a style admirably fitted to this end. Popular in the best sense, it took advantage of all the new richness of the language. His diction was racy and vivid, thronged with proverbial phrases, the slang of the streets, bold compounds, robust Saxon epithets, and metaphors drawn from English ports and countryside. The structure of his sentences reveals the growing tendencies of the time — the passionate delight in fullness of expression, the free use of doublets and alliteration, the building up of parallel constructions for the sake of rhythm. Perhaps his greatest gift, that which more than any other accounts for the freshness and vigor of his work, was one which he shared with the dramatists of his day. He had an extraordinary eye for specific detail. Whenever possible he substituted a concrete image for an abstraction, a verb that carried the picture of an action for a general statement. The result was an increased liveliness, a heightened dramatic pitch that often carried the words into a realm of imagination and feeling unsuggested by the original. Theoretically there may be no defense for such a method of translating, but in practice it succeeded as no other method could. For it made the foreign classics rich with English associations; it took Plutarch and Montaigne deep into the national consciousness.

My study of this Elizabethan art has been limited to works in prose. The reason is that the translations in verse naturally present a wholly different problem in

technique, and are, as a whole, distinctly inferior to those in prose. The barriers of meter are not easily crossed from one language into another, and it requires a poet to translate a poet. Such works as Golding's *Ovid* and Harington's *Ariosto* neither suggest the qualities of the original, nor possess exceptional poetic merit in compensation. The prose translations, on the other hand, though frequently just as far from the spirit of their originals, carry a rich and distinguished style of their own. Not even Chapman's *Homer* can rank with North's *Plutarch*. The one is an amazing *tour de force* reproducing Homer's matter with great vigor; the other is a masterpiece in its own right. We read Chapman only if we are unable to read the original. We might know Greek well and still prefer North; for his book shows a bold energy and a wealth of diction not suggested by the Greek and wholly the product of the translator's age.

Among the translations in prose, my study is further limited to five of the most important, Hoby's *Courtier*, North's *Plutarch*, Florio's *Montaigne*, and Holland's *Livy* and *Suetonius*. This choice is not wholly arbitrary, for these books represent the scope of the entire field. They extend chronologically from *The Courtier* in 1561 to the *Suetonius* in 1606, and so embrace the whole reign of Elizabeth. Further than this, each serves to illustrate certain phases of the coming of the Renaissance to England. Castiglione's *Courtier* represents

many sides of the Italian contribution to this movement, as the spirit of Montaigne's *Essays* reveals the influence of France. The important part played by the classics of Greece and Rome is suggested by the work of North and Holland. Other translations of this period, such as William Adlington's version of *The Golden Asse* of Apuleius or Thomas Underdowne's *Aethiopian Historie of Heliodorus*, rank very high as examples of rare prose, but did not exercise anything like as great a sphere of influence. Other powerful factors in the Renaissance, such as the works of Cicero and Seneca, Boccaccio and Rabelais, were not so relevant to my purpose as the works chosen, either because the translations are not so fine, or because they fall outside of the period. The greatest of all the translations of the time, and the greatest translation in the language, has also been omitted, since the long line of tradition, and the earlier work by men like Tyndale which paved the way for its achievement, are fully known.

In short, the plan has been to suggest the qualities of Elizabethan translations, their purpose and importance, by detailed analysis of a representative group. None of the books dealt with here is a translation in the modern sense of a literal word-for-word mirroring of the original. The chief consideration for Holland or North was not a meticulous imitation of the classical style, but the production of a book that would strike into the minds of their countrymen. So they bent their whole attention to

naturalizing the qualities of the original, and bringing them out to the full for the English reader. They were ready to interpolate explanations of unfamiliar allusions, and to modernize classical customs when they seemed obscure. Under their treatment Livy and Plutarch are not left foreign classics: they are brought into the main tide of English literature. To indicate the ways by which this was accomplished is the chief purpose of this book.

CHAPTER II

Hoby's Courtier

(1561)

I

SIR Thomas Hoby's translation of *The Courtier*
brought to England the ripe harvest of the Italian
Renaissance. It did not bring the Italy of Machiavelli,
or the gay sensual world of the *novelle*, or the sinister
strain of lust and intrigue that became the Italy of the
Elizabethan dramatists. Both Machiavelli and Castiglione had created ideal men. But the temper of *The
Prince* could not be appreciated in the North. The
subtle mind that, with an apparently callous indiffer-
ence to morality, followed logic to its relentless conclusion, became a thing of horror, and the vulgarized figure
of Machiavel stalked the English stage as the incarna-
tion of all evil. With *The Courtier* the situation was
very different. Hoby's translation, which appeared in
1561 — five years before William Painter's *Palace of
Pleasure* had given England the first collection of the
much decried novelists — embodied all the light and
splendor of the new spirit.

Roger Ascham and the serious English humanists de-
plored the vogue of "the merry bookes of Italie."[1] But

[1] Ascham, *The Scholemaster* (1570), ed. Arber (London, 1870), p. 79.

they had only praise for Hoby's work, in spite of the fact that the pages of *The Courtier* are freely sprinkled with idle jests and stories containing the same objectionable material. The reason for their inconsistency lay in Castiglione's high idealism, which gave breadth and color to their own. The English mind had been absorbed in erecting new ideals. Early in the century Sir Thomas More had formulated his concept of the ideal state; in the generation before Hoby, Elyot had written *The Boke of the Governour* (1531), a treatise on education calculated to produce ideal men; and in 1570 Ascham was to follow with his *Scholemaster*. But the difference between the work of these English humanists and *Il Cortegiano* is profound. It is the difference between a highly cultivated society and one whose development has just begun. At the outset of Elizabeth's reign the Renaissance in England was still an intellectual concept; it hardly touched the pulse of daily existence. The emphasis of the humanists was upon the training of character; they advocated the study of Greek for a fuller perception of the qualities that determine a good life. They were men of serious purpose, and in the purely intellectual quality of their work lay its sterility. In the middle of the sixteenth century England was, as a whole, crude and unawakened. The scholars had done their work well, but they were not artists. The imagination of the country was still waiting to be stirred.

The society in which Castiglione's ideal courtier moves is one of refinement in manners and ease in speech. Guidobaldo, Duke of Urbino, and his Duchess, Elizabeth Gonzaga, were contemporaries of Michaelangelo and Raphael; they lived in a palace that was one of the most beautiful creations of the Renaissance; and they assembled there the most cultivated and distinguished court in Italy. Count Baldessare Castiglione was in the service of the duke from 1504 until the latter's death in 1508. *Il Cortegiano*, begun while the memories of that court were fresh in his mind, unites the medieval conception of the knight with the new ideal of the scholar-gentleman. Such a figure appealed not only to the English humanists, but to the nation as a whole.

The Courtier, as an ethical and philosophical treatise on education, recommended itself highly to a man of Ascham's spirit. Its discussion of virtues was Aristotelian. Its final pages were devoted to a magnificent discourse on Platonic love. Furthermore, it dealt with many of the subjects that chiefly occupied the humanists' minds: the relation between writing and speech, the use of archaisms and new words, the comparative worth of the two sexes, and the education of women.

To ioyne learnyng with cumlie exercises [Ascham wrote] *Conto Baldasaer Castiglione*, in his booke, *Cortegiano*, doth trimlie teache: which booke, advisedlie read, and diligentlie folowed, but one year at home in England, would do a yong ientleman more good, I wisse, then three yeares travell abrode spent in *Italie*. And I mervell this booke is no more read in the

Court, than it is, seyng it is so well translated into English by a worthie Ientlemen, Syr. *Th. Hobbie*, who was many wayes well furnished with learnyng, and very expert in knowledge of divers tonges.[1]

Ascham must have underrated the extent to which the book was read, for the mark of *The Courtier* is constantly visible on the men of the Elizabethan age. References to it crop up everywhere. John Florio mentions "Castilion's Courtier and Guazzo his dialogues"[2] as the two books most likely to be read by anyone anxious to know a little Italian. Even Mistress Birdlime, the procuress in Dekker and Webster's *Westward Ho* (printed 1607), has heard of Castiglione, for she tartly remarks that Moll, the Italian merchant's wife, has a good city wit: "She hath read in the Italian Courtier that it is a special ornament to have skill in painting." Indeed Castiglione's name seems to have become a synonym for his creation, since Marston, both in his *Satires* (1598) and in *The Malcontent* (printed 1604), describes a ceremonious courtier as "the absolute Castilio."[3] These references indicate how the names of both book and author grew to be popular catchwords.

---

[1] *Ibid.*, p. 66.

[2] Florio's *Second Frutes* (1591), dedication.

[3] Castiglione's Christian name was put to a similar use in Edward Guilpin's *Skialethia, or A Shadow of Truth in certain Epigrams and Satyres* (1598):

> "Come to the court, and Balthazer affords
> Fountains of holy and rose-water words."

Marston also gave his "spruce courtier" in *Antonio and Mellida* (printed 1602) the name of Castilio Balthazar.

But they make *The Courtier* sound like one of the many manuals on etiquette that followed in its wake, and by no means indicate the scope of its influence. Neither does Ben Jonson's remark in his *Discoveries* — pertinent though it is — that life is added to writing by "pretty sayings, similitudes, and conceits, allusions from known history, or other common place, such as are in the *Courtier*, and the second book of Cicero *de oratore*." [1] For *The Courtier* was one of the key-books of the English Renaissance. Hoby's translation, first printed in 1561, passed through new editions in 1577, 1588, and 1603. And to realize how seriously the book was read it is necessary only to know that a Latin translation by Bartholomew Clerke, issued in 1571, achieved an even greater popularity than Hoby's work, reaching its sixth edition by 1612. [2]

English readers found in *The Courtier* many of the idealistic theories of the humanists, but given new warmth and substance by Castiglione's art. It provided an actual philosophy of life for the Elizabethan gentleman. A reading of its pages fitted him for the full assimilation of the elaborate refinements of the new Renaissance society. It furnished his imagination with

[1] Jonson, *Works*, ed. Gifford and Cunningham (London, 1875), IX, 210. Castiglione took a great part of his second book, *Of merie Jestes and Pranckes*, directly from Cicero.

For references to and borrowings from *The Courtier*, see M. A. Scott, *Elizabethan Translations from the Italian* (New York, 1916), pp. 446 ff.

[2] The editions are dated 1571, 1577 (the year of Hoby's second edition), 1585, 1593, 1603 (the year of Hoby's fourth edition), 1612.

the symbol of a completely developed individual, an individual who united ethical theory with spontaneity and
richness of character. That such a symbol was what the
Elizabethans wanted is manifest from the lives of their
own great men. Sir Philip Sidney stands for posterity
as the very epitome of "The Courtier," the model on
which the book might have been written.

That the men of Sidney's time felt Castiglione's book
to be an integral part of their lives is made evident by
Gabriel Harvey's copy of Hoby's translation.[1] Harvey
may have been a pedant, but he prided himself on being
a scholar-gentleman, and the heavily scored pages reveal that he lived with this volume. His first annota-
tion is dated 1572, when he was twenty-two, and there-
after they stretch intermittently over a period of more
than eighteen years. Passages are marked with a
flourish, pages are covered with signs — many of them
incomprehensible, some of them resembling the scrib-
blings of a schoolboy, as when an arrow running from
the precept "to be portly and aimiable in countenance
unto whoso behouldeth him" points to a comic sketch.
Harvey also filled the margins with Greek and Latin
quotations, with brief and pregnant digests of passages,
and with comments of his own. He took remarks of the
author and used them for caustic reflections on his

[1] See C. Ruutz-Rees, *Some Notes of Gabriel Harvey's in Hoby's Translation of Castiglione's Courtier*, Publications of the Modern Language Association (1910), XXV, 608–639.

enemies. He wrote the names of Musidorus and Pyrocles, the two brave knights of the *Arcadia*, beside Castiglione's list of faithful friends. He showed his agreement with an enthusiasm of his day by putting after the recommendation to gentlewomen "to be seene in the most necessary languages," the words "The Queen" — although he coupled her with Cleopatra.

But most significant in revealing the place that *The Courtier* held in England is the way Harvey instinctively measured his own contemporaries against Castiglione's ideal standard. He often held up John Astley as the "perfect patterne" [1] of the courtier — John Astley, Elizabeth's versatile Master of the Jewel House, whose accomplishments ranged from the authorship of an expert treatise on *The Art of Riding* to an intimate friendship with the learned Ascham.[2] Harvey also marked the great name of Sir Thomas More against the passage which recounts how the courtier in jesting and laughing "hath in him a certaine sweetenesse, and so comely demeanours, that whoso speaketh with him or yet be-

---

[1] Harvey repeated his comment in *Pierce's Supererogation:* "I cannot forget the gallant discourse of Horsemanship penned by a rare gentleman, M. John Asteley of the Court, whom I dare intitle our English Xenophon, and marvell not that Pietro Bizzaro, a learned Italian, proposeth him for a perfect Patterne of Castilio's Courtier." *Works*, ed. Grosart (London, 1884), II, 99.

[2] Astley was a guest at the dinner party cited in the preface to *The Scholemaster.* One of Harvey's notes reads: "M. Ascham wrote his Discourse of Germane Affayeres to this M. Astely; whereby it appearith that they had red togither Aristotle's Rhetorique, Tully, and Livy."

holdeth him, muste nedes beare him an affection for-
ever." [1]

But *The Courtier* was not only the greatest single instrument in shaping the new conception of the gentleman. It was not only a treatise on education, but a work
of art. The great poets felt its power. Spenser's purpose in *The Faerie Queene* is not far removed from
Castiglione's. He states in his preface that he hopes "to
fashion a gentleman or noble person in vertuous and
gentle discipline," and his method is to inculcate "the
twelve private moral vertues" of Aristotle by their representation in the lives of twelve knights. In addition,
it has been pointed out [2] that when Spenser sang his
"Hymne in Honour of Beautie," a most likely source
from which he could have taken his matter was the
Platonic oration of Cardinal Bembo in Castiglione's
final pages.

Certain sentences in the first book strike the reader
with a strange familiarity:

And forsomuch as our mindes are very apte to love and to
hate: as in the sightes of combates and games and in all other
kinde of contencion one with an other, it is seene that the
lookers on many times beare affeccion without any manifest
cause why, unto one of the two parties, with a gredy desire to
have him get the victorie, and the other to have the over-
throw.

[1] Hoby also, in one of his marginal notes, remarks on More's excellence in
jests. See *The Courtier*, Tudor Translations, ed. W. Raleigh (London, 1900),
p. 169. All page references are to this edition.

[2] By G. Wyndham, in his introduction to *The Poems of Shakespeare*
(London, 1898), pp. cxix–cxxi.

It seems impossible that they did not lurk in Marlowe's memory when he wrote the superb passage in *Hero and Leander:*

> It lies not in our power to love, or hate,
> For will in us is over-rul'd by fate.
> When two are stript long ere the course begin,
> We wish that one should loose, the other win;
> And one especiallie doe we affect
> Of two gold Ingots like in each respect.
> The reason no man knowes, let it suffise,
> What we behold is censur'd by our eies.
> Where both deliberat, the love is slight.
> Who ever lov'd, that lov'd not at first sight?

It must not be forgotten that when Hoby translated Castiglione's subtle dialogue and sparkling play of wit upon wit, the great English drama was still to be born. How substantial a part the form of *The Courtier* played in determining that of Elizabethan comedy can be only conjectured, but the forerunners of Shakespeare could have had at their disposal no dialogue more smooth, light, and swiftly moving than that embodying these imaginary conversations at the Court of Urbino. And in the repartee between that witty misogynist Lord Gaspare Pallavicino and the charming and no less witty Lady Emilia Pia, one constantly thinks of the merry war of Beatrice and Benedick.[1]

---

[1] See Mary A. Scott, *The Book of the Courtyer: A Possible Source of Benedick and Beatrice*, Publications of the Modern Language Association (1901), XVI, 475–502. Miss Scott goes too far in virtually asserting that Lord Gaspare and Lady Emilia *are* Shakespeare's characters. The temper is very similar, but there is no sign of direct influence.

II

It has been necessary to travel so far afield in order to suggest how widely *The Courtier* was felt in Elizabethan life. Its translator, Sir Thomas Hoby, was himself an excellent embodiment of Castiglione's ideal. Born in 1530, the younger son of William Hoby of Leominster, he went up to St. John's College, Cambridge, at the age of fifteen. This was the time of St. John's greatest glory. She was the light of the University in both learning and Protestant theology, as is revealed by the later eloquent tribute in Ascham's *Scholemaster*. That "Exchequer of Eloquence, Sir John Cheke, a man of men, supernaturally traded in all tongues," [1] was the leading spirit. Ascham himself was about to be made Public Orator. Young Hoby came under the spell of these great men, but after two years' work he left Cambridge to travel on the Continent and learn foreign languages with a view to a diplomatic career.

The account of his wanderings and of the chief subsequent events that befell him has been preserved in *A Booke of the Travaile and Lief of Me Thomas Hoby*.[2] The fascination of this journal is great; for it records the impressions of an alert young man with the whole pag-

[1] This is Nashe's tribute, in his preface to Greene's *Menaphon* (1589), which reveals how the tradition of Cheke's greatness lasted in the next generation.

[2] This was finally printed by the Camden Society in 1902 from the manuscript in the British Museum (The Camden Miscellany, X, ii, ed. E. Powell).

eant of Europe spread out before him. Properly enough, he went directly to the Protestant center at Strassburg, where, as the guest of the notable Martin Bucer, he remained for a year, studying theology and the classics. His first literary work was undertaken here at the age of eighteen — a translation of a Latin treatise of his host's: "The gratulation of the mooste famous clerk M. Bucer, a man of no lesse learning and lyterature then Godlye Studie and example of lyving, unto the Church of England, for the restitution of Christes religion."

By the summer of 1548 Hoby's brother held an appointment as Ambassador to the Emperor, with residence at Augsburg, and after a short visit there, Thomas set out for Italy. He was a student for a time at the University of Padua. He stayed long in Venice, and although he witnessed with his own eyes an incident in the feud between the families of Della Torre and Soveragnani which resulted in the murder of the head of the latter house, he did not react to it with the horror felt by Ascham, who in his nine days in this "Circe's court" saw more evil than he ever heard of in London within nine years. For Hoby was capable of appreciating the sensuous splendor of the city, then in the Indian summer of its glory, with Titian in full career and Tintoretto producing his gorgeous masterpieces for the School of St. Roch.

At Shroftide after [Hoby records] there came to Venice to see the citie the lustie yong Duke of Ferrandin, well accompanied with noble menn and gentlemen, where he and his companions in Campo di San Stefano shewed great sport and muche pastime to the gentlmen & gentlwomen of Venice, bothe on horsback in running at the ring with faire Turks and Cowrsars, being in a maskerie after the Turkishe maner, and on foote casting of eggs into the wyndowes among the ladies full of sweete waters and damaske poulders.[1]

He feels the full charm of this, even though his next sentence must add:

At night after all this triumph in a bankett, made purposlie at Mowrano, a little owt of Venice, by the Seniorye, to honor him withall, he was slaine by a varlett belonging to a gentleman of the citie.

Ascham, in recommending the reading of *The Courtier* as being worth more than a three years' stay in Italy, seems to have forgotten that its translator acquired his skill in divers tongues only through considerably more than three years abroad, and that the book itself grew out of such subtlety and refinement as existed in Venice side by side with its lust and cruelty.

Hoby also attended the reception in Venice of the Duke and Duchess of Urbino, on the day of the annual ceremony of the Bucentoro, when the Doge married his city to the Adriatic.[2] Like all scholarly travelers of his

---

[1] *A Booke of the Travaile and Lief of Me*, p. 14.

[2] Remembrance of this scene caused Hoby to make this note on the Bucentoro at p. 165 of his translation of *The Courtier:* "A faire vessell of pleasure in Venice made Galliwise. Every year upon the Ascension daye the Duke with all the counsell goith in it a mile or two into the sea, and there casteth a ring of gold into it thinking by this yearly ceremonye they so marie the Sea that it will never leave the Citye on drie lande."

time he was eager to visit every monument, and to record fully the inscriptions and epitaphs. His memory dwelt on the heroes of classic tradition, and was always stocked with what Livy, Suetonius, or Plutarch had said about the spot he was visiting. His pages are filled with vivid pictures of social history. He traveled south, through Florence and Siena to Rome, where he waited some weeks in order to witness the election of a new pope. But such an interest did not prevent him from later remarking on the "fond folishnes" of papistry that let people believe that Saint Agatha's body in the church at Catania kept Aetna from erupting.[1]

The tone and even the words of his journal are often amusingly like that of the English undergraduate of to-day: "After Mr. Barker, Mr. Parker, Whitehorn and I had throwghlie searched owt such antiquities as were here to bee seene from place to place . . . we thowght it but losse of time to make anie longer abode here." [2] And so they took ship from Rome to Naples, and were informed upon their arrival that, if they had chanced to come by day instead of by night, they would certainly have been set upon by Moors and Turks, and "bine all taken slaves." [3] Hoby has the highest praise for the wines of Naples, and the description of his reception by the Marquis of Capistrano at Amalfi reveals in a sentence the development of Italian housekeeping to a level then undreamt of in England:

[1] p. 47.   [2] p. 25.   [3] p. 27.

When suppar was done everie mann was browght to his rest: Whitehorn and I were had into a chamber hanged with clothe of gold and vellett, wherein were two beddes, th' on of silver worke and the other of vellett, with pillowes bolsters and the shetes curiouslie wrowght with neelde [needle] worke.[1]

When he had seen Naples thoroughly, Hoby decided to go alone through the dukedom of Calabria into Sicily, both to have a sight of the country and also to absent himself for a while from Englishmen's company "for the tung's sake."[2] Finally he headed north, and in the summer of 1550, two years after his original departure, he rejoined his brother at Augsburg. During his stay there he occupied himself with another translation, this time an Italian morality play, *The Tragedie of Free Will*,[3] the theme of which is that the pope is the true Antichrist. Twenty years old, he had now completed his education. In the company of his brother, Sir Philip, he traveled home by way of Antwerp, and was presented at the court of Edward VI on Christmas day.

His first appointment followed immediately. He was attached to the train of the Marquis of Northampton, and went with him to Chateaubriand to assist at the presentation of the Order of the Garter to Henry II. The next years were spent mainly abroad. In the autumn of 1552 his journal records:

After I had convayed my stuff to Paris and settled myself there, the first thing I did was to translate into Englishe the

---

[1] p. 54.   [2] p. 37.

[3] *Tragedia di F. N.* [*egri*] *B.* [*assanese*] *intitolita, Libero Arbitrio* (1546).

third booke of the Cowrtisan which my Ladie Marquess had often willed me to do, and for lacke of time ever differred it. And from thense I sent unto Sir Henry Sidney the epitome of the Italian tung which I drue owt there for him. This done Mr. Henry Kingsmeale and I applied ourselves to the reading of the institutes of the Civill Law, being bothe lodged in a house together.[1]

The accession of Catholic Mary was a check to the Hobys' active career. They went away from England for some months, nominally for Sir Philip to take the cure at the baths of Göppingen and Caldiero, and for Thomas to profit by contact with Sir John Cheke, Sir Anthony Cooke, and other distinguished exiles at Padua. On their return home, they lived in retirement on their estate at Bisham. Sir Philip died in May, 1558, and in the same year Thomas was married to Elizabeth Cooke, one of the gifted daughters of Sir Anthony. The remainder of the journal is chiefly taken up with an account of the improvements made to his house, of the children born to him, and of the distinguished visitors he entertained.

Under Queen Elizabeth Hoby was in great favor. He was knighted in March, 1566, and directly afterwards was appointed Her Majesty's Ambassador to the King of France. His journey was not auspicious. He was delayed in Calais by a dispute occasioned by a French soldier's having "with his arequebuse shott through oure flagg in two places, in the read crosse and in the whit

[1] p. 78.

about it." [1] He proceeded to Paris not without foreboding over this "hard beginning." He was presented to the king, undertook the routine duties of his post, but on July 13 died suddenly, at the age of thirty-six. His body was conveyed to Bisham, and Queen Elizabeth wrote a letter of condolence to his wife.

III

It is not quite certain when the other three books of *The Courtier* were added to the translation Hoby had made in Paris of the section concerning "the condiciouns and qualities of a waytinge gentillwoman." An entry in his journal during his second stay in Padua reads, "The writing began the xviii[th] of November 1554 I ended the ix[th] of Februarie followinge." [2] If this refers to the work by which his name lives to-day, it was accomplished before he was twenty-five. At all events it seems to have been finished by 1556, since "The Epistle of the Translator" was dated in that year. In this preface Hoby explains that he forbore and lingered a great while

to see if anye of a more perfect understanding in the tunge, and better practised in the matter of the booke (of whom we want not a number in this realm) would take the matter in hande, to do his countrey so great a benefite: and this imagination prevailed in me a long space after my duetie done in translating the thirde booke . . . in that I was enfourmed, it was as then in some great forwardness by another, whose wit

[1] State Papers, Foreign, of April 9, 1566.   [2] p. 119.

and stile was greatly to be allowed, but sins prevented by death he could not finish it. But of late beeyng instantly craved upon a fresh, I whetted my stile and settled myself to take in hand the other three books.

The translation thus completed was not put into print until five years later. In the fall of 1560 an entry in Hoby's journal — "The v of November I removed from Bissham to London, and there remained xiii weeks"[1] — coincides with the time of the book's passing through the press, and doubtless accounts for the comparative absence of misprints. The reason for the long delay is hinted at darkly by the printer:

Certain places in it . . . of late yeares beeing misliked of some that had the perusing of it (with what reason judge thou) the Author thought it much better to keepe it in darknes a while, then to put it in light unperfect and in peecemeale to serve the time.[2]

This means simply that the freedom of certain of Castiglione's anecdotes about the clergy, which had not offended Leo X or Clement VII, was looked upon in a very different light by the Papist party in England, as it was by the Counter-Reformation in Italy,[3] once the

[1] p. 128.   [2] "The Printer to the Reader."

[3] Raleigh, in his introduction, cites some amusing examples of the way the book was expurgated by the Abate Pierantonio Serassi in his Italian edition of 1766. Raphael's remark to two cardinals (Hoby, p. 184) that he has painted Saint Peter and Saint Paul with such red faces because of their shame at the corruption of the clergy, is assigned to an anonymous artist of ancient Rome; and the blushes become those of Romulus and Remus. The foolish countryman who compared his venerable goat to Saint Paul (Hoby, p. 163), is made to find a more seemly comparison in the person of Socrates.

supremacy of the old Church had been challenged. So the book of the devout Catholic Castiglione had to delay its appearance in England until the reign of the Protestant Elizabeth.

At the time when Hoby wrote, there was a growing conviction among his countrymen that translation was a work of patriotism.[1] In 1539 Richard Taverner had declared that he had been incited to put part of the *Chiliades* of Erasmus into English by the love he bore "to the furtherance and adornment"[2] of his native country. Nicholas Udall, the author of *Ralph Roister Doister*, stressed the national and social importance of such work in the dedication of his *Paraphrase upon the Newe Testamente* (1549), stating that "a translator travaileth not to his own private commodity, but to the benefit and public use of his country." Nicholas Grimald's endeavor in turning Cicero into English (1558) was to do for his countrymen what "Italians, Frenchmenne, Spaniards, Dutchmen, and other foreigns have liberally done for theirs."[3] The increasing desire was for England to have an equal share with other lands in letters as well as in commerce and voyaging. John Brende echoed

[1] Flora R. Amos, *Early Theories of Translation*, Columbia University Studies (New York, 1920), contains valuable material from the dedications and prefaces of translators from King Alfred to Pope, but is put together rather mechanically.

[2] In his prologue to *Proverbs or Adagies gathered out of the Chiliades of Erasmus* (1539).

[3] The statement to the reader, prefixed to *Cicero's three bookes of dueties* (1558).

the popular voice when he presented Quintus Curtius'
History of Alexander the Great (1553) in the hope "that
we Englishmen might be found as forward in that be-
half as other nations, which have brought all worthy histories into their natural language." [1]

The feeling prevailed that these new books would
have a direct bearing upon daily life, that they would
bring new blood and vigor to the stock of England.
Richard Eden remarked, in the preface to his translation from the Spanish of Martin Cortés' *Arte de Navigar*
(1561), "Nowe therefore this worke of the art of Navi-
gation beyng publyshed in our vulgar tongue, you may
be assured to have more store of skylful Pilotes." Hel-
lowes insisted on the practical use of Guevara's *Familiar
Epistles* (1574), since they teach "rules for Kinges to
rule, counsellers to counsell, prelates to practise, captaines to execute, soldiers to performe, the married to
followe, the prosperous to prosecute, and the poore in
adversitie to bee comforted . . . how to write or talke
with all men, in all matters at large" [2] — an insistence
which reveals in its rhetoric that the art of advertising
was not undiscovered. Thomas Wilson's serious purpose
in translating *Three Orations of Demosthenes* (1570) is
more clearly seen through his blunt statement on the
title-page that they are "most needful to be read in
these dangerous days of all them that love their country's libertie."

---

[1] In his dedication.   [2] In his preface, "To the Reader."

Hoby shared the belief that a man's reading shapes the course of his life. He realized England's inferiority to the Continent in learning; he knew that *The Courtier* had long since been translated into Spanish and French.[1] He had also felt its power, and as he expresses it, "Many most excellent wittes in this realme have made no lesse of this boke then the Great Alexander did of Homer."[2] So he considered that he had performed a national service of no small magnitude when he could write: "But nowe, though late in deede, yet for al that at length, beside his three principal languages, in the which he hath a long time haunted all the Courtes of Christendome, hee is become an Englishman."[3] For Hoby thought that the reason England lagged behind other countries was simply owing to the fact that where foreigners

set their delite and bende themselves with an honest strife of matching others, to tourne into their mother tunge, not onely the wittie writinges of other languages, but also of all the Philosophers, and all Sciences both Greeke and Latin, our men weene it sufficient to have a perfecte knowledge, to no other ende, but to profite themselves, and (as it were) after much paynes in breaking up a gap, bestow no lesse to close it up againe, that others maye with like travaile folowe after.[4]

In opposition to the old objection, which Hoby stated to be the prevailing academic opinion of his day, that not

[1] The first Spanish version was that by Boscán (Barcelona, 1534). J. Colin's French version appeared in Paris in 1538. L. Opdycke, in his translation of *The Courtier* (New York, 1901) gives a bibliography of the editions in Italian, French, Spanish, Latin, English, and German, listing 143 editions, 105 of them earlier than 1603.

[2] "The Epistle of the Translator," p. 8.   [3] p. 5.   [4] p. 8.

to leave the classics in the original "hurteth memorie
and hindreth learning," [1] he and Wilson [2] and the other
democratic followers of Cheke believed that "where the
Sciences are most tourned into the vulgar tunge, there
are the best learned men." [3]

Hoby also came to his work with a definite theory of
translation. He sharply rejected the medieval practice
of following the author comfortably, sometimes word for
word, sometimes according to the sense. This had not
only been King Alfred's theory as expressed in the preface to his version of *The Pastoral Care*; it had persisted
through Caxton into the sixteenth century. Alexander
Barclay translated *The Ship of Fools* (1508), not for the
learned to judge its correctness, but "to clense the
vanyte and madnes of folysshe people." Consequently,
though following in general the "sentence" of his author, he did not scruple sometimes to add details, sometimes to take away such things as seemed to him superfluous.[4] Barclay's contemporary, Lord Berners, said of

---

[1] p. 8.

[2] In the "Epistle to Sir William Cecil" prefaced to his *Three Orations of
Demosthenes*, Wilson wrote in defense of translation: "Indede my labor can
be no hurt to anybody, except it be to my selfe. For the Greeke is as it was,
and those that were Grecians may read the Greke still notwithstanding my
English. . . . But such as are grieved, with translated bokes, are lyke to
them that eating fine Manchet, are angry with others that feede on Cheate
breade. And yet God knoweth men would as gladly eate Manchet as they, if
they had it. But all can not weare Velvet, or feede with the best, and therefore such are contented for necessities sake to weare our Countrie cloth, and
to take themselves to harde fare, that can have no better."   [3] p. 8.

[4] "But concernynge the translacion of this Boke: I exhort ye reders to
take no displesour for it is not translated word by worde according to the

his own translation of Froissart: "And in that I have not followed myne authour worde by worde, yet I trust I have ensewed the true reporte of the sentence of the mater." [1]

The translator of *The Courtier* took no such freedom with his text. The new learning had brought a new perception of the value of faithfulness to the original. The poet Nicholas Grimald stated at length the humanists' position in the preface to his *Cicero* (1558):

> Howbeit loke, what rule the Rhetorician gives in precept, to be observed of an Oratour, in telling of his tale: that it be short, and without ydle words: that it be plain, and without dark sense: that it be provable, and without any swarving from the trouthe: the same rule should be used in examining, and judging of a translation. For if it be not as brief, as the verie authors text requireth: whatso is added to his perfite stile, shal appere superfluous, and to serve rather to the making of some paraphrase, or commentarie. Thereto, if it be uttered with ynkehorne termes, and not with usuall wordes: or if it be phrased with wrasted or farrefetched fourmes of speeche: not fine, but harshe, not easie, but hard, not natural, but violent it shal seme to be. Then also, in case it yelde not the meaning of the author; but eyther following fansie, or misledde by errour, forsakes the true pattern: it cannot be approved for a faithful, and sure interpretacioun: which ought to be taken for the greatest praise of all.

This passage shows the mark of Wilson's *Art of Rhetorike*, which had appeared in 1551. Wilson himself, in

---

verses of my actour. For I have but only drawen into our moder tunge, in rude language the sentences of the verses as nere as the parcyte of my wyt wyl suffer me, sometyme addynge, sometyme detractinge and takinge away suche thinges as semeth me [un] necessary and superflue." *The Ship of Fools*, ed. T. H. Jamieson (Edinburgh, 1874), "The Argument," p. 17.

[1] *The Chronicle of Froissart*, ed. W. P. Ker (London, 1901), "The Preface of the Translator."

dedicating his *Demosthenes* (1570) to Cheke's brother-in-law, Sir William Cecil, with eloquent tribute to his dead master,[1] observed like principles.

But perhaps [he wrote] whereas I have been somewhat curious to followe Demosthenes' natural phrase, it may be thought that I doe speake over bare Englysh. Well I had rather follow his veine, the which was to speake simple and plainly to the common people's understanding, than to over flouryshe wyth superfluous speach, although I might thereby be counted equal with the best that ever wrote English.[2]

A decade earlier Hoby had struck the same note:

I have endevoured my self to folow the very meaning and woordes of the Author, without being misled by fansie, or leaving out any percell one or other, whereof I knowe not how some of the interpreters of this booke into other languages can excuse themselves, and the more they be conferred, the more it will perchaunce appeere.[3]

How completely he considered himself a disciple of Cheke's is revealed by "A Letter of Syr J. Cheekes to his loving frind Mayster Thomas Hoby" inserted at the beginning of *The Courtier*. Hoby had sent him his work, and Cheke is returning it with praise, having at the young man's request bestowed especial attention upon the preface and taken the liberty of changing certain

---

[1] "Master Cheke's judgment was great in translating out of one tongue into another, and better skill he had in our English speech to judge of the Phrases and properties of wordes, and to divide sentences than any else that I have known."

[2] In his preface, "To the Reader."

[3] "The Epistle of the Translator," p. 11. The last part of this sentence reveals that Hoby had fulfilled the task of a good translator by comparing the various editions. Colin's French version has many omissions.

words. It was in this letter that Cheke gave utterance to his famous dictum as a purist:

I am of this opinion that our own tung shold be written cleane and pure, unmixt and unmangeled with borowing of other tungs, wherein if we take not heed by tiim, ever borrowing and never payeng, she shall be fain to keep her house as bankrupt.

His metaphor, which adroitly confuses language and economics, is not intended to reprove Hoby, who had "scarslie and necessarily used whear occasion serveth a strange word or so, as it seemeth to grow out of the matter and not to be sought for." Fortunately, however, Hoby had given himself greater liberty than his master prescribed. Though he often wrote a crude Saxon idiom, no misplaced sense of nationalism caused him to reject loan words in favor of some of the strange terms that sprinkle Cheke's *New Testament*. Cheke and the purists did a service to the language in preserving many good Old English words against the onslaught of the Latinists, but that their theory was impossibly limited becomes too clear when we read, in *St. Matthew*, "frosent" for "apostles," or "biwordes" instead of "parables." [1]

Hoby's *Courtier* was dedicated fittingly to Lord Henry Hastings, whose grandfather had entertained

---

[1] Other examples are "wiseards" for the Authorized Version's "wise men," "moond" for lunaticke," "tollers" for "publicans," "ground wrought" for "founded," "hunderder" for "centurion," "freschman" for "proselyte." See Cheke's *St. Matthew*, ed. J. Goodwin (London, 1843).

Castiglione when he came to London to receive from Henry VII the Order of the Garter for the Duke of Urbino, and for himself a carcanet of price. In addition to Cheke's letter, the book was prefaced with a commendatory sonnet by Thomas Sackville, and is thus shown to have been highly esteemed by the translator's most distinguished contemporaries. But Hoby himself was modest. He had undertaken the task because he felt the high necessity of Castiglione's book for every gentleman of the court. But he had also felt the smooth richness of the original, and was obliged to confess: "My smalle understandyng in the tung, and less practise in the matters herein conteined, is not of force to give it the brightness and full perfection in this our tung that it hath in the Italian." [1]

IV

In keeping with the declaration of his preface, Hoby follows his author very closely. Frequently the words are different, but leave the sense the same: as, "But truely I would with all my hearte bee ridde of this burthen" [2] for "Ma io veramente molto volentier fuggirei questa fatica." [3] Occasionally the translation is not so full as the original, but more often it is a little fuller. Hoby introduces a few words to make his meaning

[1] "The Epistle of the Translator," p. 10.

[2] p. 43.

[3] Castiglione, *Il Cortegiano*, ed. O. Bacci, Istituto Editorale Italiano (Milan, 1914), p. 50. Page references are always to this edition.

clearer, or adds phrases that bring greater strength to the feeling and round out the swing of his prose, as when he writes "But not as those lustie laddes dooe, that open their mouthe and thruste out woordes at aventure *they care not how*" [1] for the more restrained "Ma non di quella maniera che fanno questi bravi, che aprono la bocca, e lassano venir le parole alla ventura." [2]

But in general Hoby stays even too close to the Italian. It is true that his knowledge of the language was far from perfect, and when he had not fully understood the sense he did his best by following his author word for word. As a result "lampi e saette" [3] becomes "twincklinges and sperkeles," [4] when what is meant is "lightning and thunderbolts." Where Hoby causes Unico Aretino to call the duchess "a most perfect mere-mayden" [5] instead of "verissima Sirena," [6] and then to remark on the "S" she wears in her forehead, he has left the word play without meaning. In another place he makes the empty remark that people object to seeing young men riding about the streets "upon mules," [7] when the word "mula" here means that they should not ride "in pumps." Again, an unthinking literal rendering causes him to describe a man on horseback "stirato in su la sella, e, come noi sogliam dire, alla veneziana" [8] as "bolt upright setled in saddle (as we used to say after the Venetian phrase)." [9] It should be "in the Venetian

---

[1] pp. 50–51.   [2] p. 58.   [3] p. 101.   [4] p. 94.   [5] p. 38.
[6] p. 45.   [7] p. 107.   [8] p. 68.   [9] p. 60.

manner," a manner Hoby ought to have remembered
well from the times he had seen Verrocchio's magnificent
equestrian statue of Colleone.

This literalism, resulting from the translator's failure
to grasp the sense, renders several passages incomprehensible. For instance, it takes some puzzling to find out
that "These defaultes that I talke of take this grace
from you" [1] really means "These weaknesses of yours I
am speaking of deprive you of grace." In the case of certain of the longer sentences it becomes almost impossible
to thread the labyrinth.[2] In addition, there are naturally
plenty of mistakes in finding the right equivalent for a
word.[3] "In a manner" regularly appears for "quasi,"
and makes some sentences very clumsy: "For (in a
maner) alwayes a manne by sundrye wayes may clime

[1] Hoby follows the Italian construction, "Questi vostri difetti di che io
parlo vi levano la grazia," p. 87.

[2] For instance, the confusion of: "Have you not read of the five daughters
of Croton, which among the rest of the people, Zeusis the peincter chose to
make of all five one figure that was most excellent in beawty, and wer re-
nowned of many Poets, as they that wer alowed for beawtifull of him that
ought to have a most perfect judgment in beawty," p. 97, for "Non avete
voi leto, che quelle cinque fanciulle da Crotone, le quali tra l'altre di quel
populo elesse Zeusi pittore, per far di tutte cinque una sola figura eccellen-
tissima di bellezza, furono celebrate da molti poeti, come quelle che per
belle erano state approvate da colui, che perfettissimo giudicio di bellezza
aver dovea?" p. 104.

[3] This is most noticeable in his lack of sureness in choosing adjectives.
For instance, the provision that the courtier's voice should be "not to subtyll or soft, as in a woman: nor yet so boysterous and roughe, as in one of the
Countrey, but shrill, clere, sweete and wel framed." "Thin," not "subtyll"
is the proper sense of "sottile"; "sonorous" not "shrill" for "sonora"; and
"well-sounding" not the vague "wel framed" for "ben composta."

to the toppe of all perfection" is rough going for the
simple idea that there are almost always more ways than
one to reach the goal. "Solemnesse" [1] is an inaccurate
rendering of "insolenzia," [2] just as "palmestrers" [3] is of
"fisionimi"; [4] and "Whoso hath grace is gracious" [5]
does not carry the pointed sense of "Chi ha grazia,
quello è grato." [6] Nor is "eleganzia," [7] the crowning
quality of the courtier's manner, fittingly rendered by
the inexpressive "easiness of understanding." [8] Even
more confusing are the cases where Hoby loses the construction of the sentence,[9] or, missing the punctuation,
divides his words wrongly.[10]

But confusion arises often, not from Hoby's lack of
mastery in Italian, but from the awkwardness of his
English. How words sometimes sprawl across his page
can be illustrated from a single sentence in Bembo's discourse on the essence of Platonic love:

And otherwhile whan the stirringe vertues of the body are
withdrawen alone through earnest beholdinge, eyther fast
bounde through sleepe, when she is not hindred by them, she
feeleth a certein previe smell of the right aungelike beawtie,
and ravished with the shining of that light, beeginneth to be

---

[1] p. 315.   [2] p. 320.   [3] p. 348.   [4] p. 353.
[5] p. 56.   [6] p. 64.   [7] p. 78.   [8] p. 70.

[9] He frequently uses a temporal conjunction when a causal is demanded:
"And whan al was whist, the L. General said," p. 98, where the sense is
"Since everyone remained silent."

[10] For instance, "With this [i. e. singing] the unmanerly countrey woman
that aryseth before daye *oute of her slepe* to spinne and carde, *defendeth her
self* and maketh her labor pleasant," p. 90, for "Con questo la inculta con-
tadinella, che inanzi al giorno a filare o a tessere si lieva, *dal sonno si difende*,
e la sua fatica fa piacevole," p. 97.

inflamed, and so greedily foloweth after, that (in a maner) she wexeth dronken and beeside her self, for coveting to coople her self with it, havinge founde (to her wening) the foote steppes of God, in the beehouldinge of whom (as in her happy end) she seeketh to settle her self." [1]

The sentence in the original is a great deal longer, but Castiglione could manage the involutions of a full compound period where Hoby stumbles hopelessly from clause to clause. His undeveloped English cannot cope with the Italian, and he only confounds confusion by his despairing parentheses.

Hoby's chief limitation is his uncertain syntax. His resolute use of native words may jar the philosophic temper of a passage, but this is nothing [2] to the havoc worked by lack of skill in handling prepositional phrases or by his confused word-order. When he writes "For beeside the three great ones that we have named, of whom may be hoped it, that beelongeth to the high degree of a perfect Prince," [3] it is only too plain that the language did not bend to his command. His grammar is frankly sketchy; he inserts modifying phrases at such places in a sentence that it is impossible to determine

---

[1] p. 359.

[2] Sometimes his purism makes a sentence awkward through lack of variety: "And their is no matter, that hath not in it many thinges of *like* sort *unlike* the one to the other, which for al that among themselves deserve a *like* praise," p. 75, for "Nè è natura alcuna che non abbia in sè molte cose della *medesima* sorte *dissimili* l'una dall' altra, le quali però son tra sè di *egual* laude degne," p. 82.

[3] The Italian reads: "Perchè, oltra quelli tre grandi che avemo nominati, dei quali sperar si po ciò che s'è detto convenirsi al supremo grado di perfetto principe," pp. 337–338.

their connection; [1] his choice of words is weak in more
than one important instance; [2] and on nearly every page
there is testimony that English prose had not yet become a faultless instrument for every kind of expression.

But the indictment against Hoby must not be made
too sweeping. He may fumble certain passages and
transform courtly Italian into uncouth English, but he
had given himself wholly to his book. He is guilty of
only a few trifling omissions, as when he abandons the
attempt to wrestle with the names of Italian dances, and
for "avendo prima danzato una bassa, ballarono una
roegarze" [3] writes simply "shewed them a daunce or
twoo." [4] And that he had considered his work thoroughly is clear from the scope and variety of his marginal notes. He explains many things for his English
readers: the nature of the tarantula; [5] that "a certayne
Philosopher" mentioned by Castiglione is Anaxagoras; [6]

[1] "To abide by" is a vigorous rendering of "certamente," but the way it
is inserted in the clause destroys its meaning: "For to abide by, whoso loseth
his conning at that time, sheweth that he hath firste loste his heart,"
p. 53.
[2] To describe an essential characteristic of the courtier by saying that he
should appear in his every action "to do it without pain, and (as it were) not
mynding it," p. 59, is wholly inadequate for "venir fatto senza fatica e
quasi senza pensarvi," p. 66.
[3] p. 107.   [4] p. 100.
[5] This explanation is particularly elaborate: "A kind of spiders, whiche
beyng dyvers of nature cause divers effectes, some after their biting fal a
singing, some laugh, some wepe, some watche, some sweate: and this disease
is onely cured with instrumentes of musick, which must never cease until the
diseased beyng constrained with the melodye thereof to fall a daunsinge with
long exercise overcometh the force of this poyson," p. 37.
[6] p. 51.

that what the Italian called "gozzuti" are "men in the mountaines with great bottles of flesh under their chin, through the drinking of snow water"; [1] that Aquapendente "is a towne of the Popes xii miles from Paglia." [2] What is more significant, he compiles at the end of the volume a full outline of "The Chiefe Conditions and Qualities in a Courtier."

Hoby shows a knowledge of the background out of which the book had grown. When the "three noble writers" of Italy are mentioned, he names them — "Petrarca, Dante, Boccaccio" [3] — and this is one of the not very numerous references to Dante in sixteenth-century England. In the second book he is aware that "this discourse of Jestes is taken out of Cicero *de Orat.* lib. ii," [4] and he also traces the material from the *Decameron* in this section to proper tale and day. [5] He knows Petrarch's sonnets, [6] and he knows the classics — not only Aristotle's *Physics*, [7] and Plutarch, [8] and Pliny's stories of famous women, [9] but also "Demosthenes answer to Lais of Corinth that asked him xxiiii li. for one night." [10] The extensiveness and pertinence of his notes on the discussion of language in the first book may

---

[1] p. 136.   [2] p. 194.   [3] p. 68.

[4] p. 153. His knowledge of *De Oratore* is apparently close, for he states at p. 159, "Cicero mentioneth not this last kind of jestes."

[5] pp. 161, 200, etc.

[6] Hoby notes that certain lines on p. 87 are from "Son. 155."

[7] He traces the saying of "a great philosopher," p. 226, to "Aristot. i. Physic. XVIII."

[8] p. 236.   [9] p. 234.   [10] p. 257.

well indicate his own interest in the subject. For such remarks as those justifying the wish "to forge new wordes," [1] and the statements that there are "thinges good in every tunge," [2] that "what is alowed in wryting, is allowed in speaking," [3] and that "men never delited in wordes worne out with time," [4] express in brief the growing practice of the Elizabethans.

And if the translator's closeness to his author sometimes causes him to write crabbedly, on other occasions the words pass through an alchemy that makes Italian into English. Such a phrase as "to hale by the haire" [5] seems wholly Elizabethan, but it is taken directly from "tirar per i capegli." [6] So with "And in this maner was one of the beste favoured and towardlyest personages in the world deformed and marred in his greene age" [7] for "E così restò un dei più belli e disposti corpi del mondo deformato e guasto nella sua verde età." [8] The sentences follow each other word for word, and yet Hoby's possesses all the freshness and vitality of an original expression. Often by the slightest twist the temper of a passage is wholly naturalized, as when "wonderous great pleasure" [9] appears for "maraviglioso piacere," [10] or "merye conceites" [11] for "oneste facezie." [12]

Throughout Hoby's book you are aware of the qualities that were to characterize the full Elizabethan

---

[1] p. 71.   [2] p. 73.   [3] p. 64.   [4] p. 69.
[5] p. 59.   [6] p. 67.   [7] p. 30.   [8] p. 38.
[9] p. 33.   [10] p. 41.   [11] p. 32.   [12] p. 40.

speech. The use of doublets in *The Courtier* is slight as compared with the later vogue, yet it appears. The Lady Emilia Pia, "la maestra di tutti," [1] is called "the maistresse and ringe leader of all the companye." [2] "Gaming and pastime," [3] "condicions and qualityes," [4] "flockes and herdes," [5] each appear in place of a single noun in Castiglione. Occasionally verbs are doubled: "Some will delite more in modestie, some other wyll *fansye* a manne that is actyve and always doynge"; [6] more often, adjectives, "soft and quiet" [7] for "placide," [8] to speak "of pleasant matters, of mery conceites, of honest divises" [9] for "di cose piacevoli, di giochi, di motti." [10] But on the whole the elaborations of the text are very few.

This restraint did not keep Hoby from writing in robust style. "Oure Courtier shall use no fonde sausinesse. He shall be no carier about of trifling newes. . . . He shall be no babbler" shows how far the book has been carried from the Court of Urbino, and yet Hoby is paralleling the constructions of his author. [11] And if the translator's sentences do not suggest Castiglione's balance and control, they have an excellent ring of their own.

[1] p. 39.　　　　[2] p. 32.　　　　[3] p. 124 ("il giocare," p. 130).
[4] p. 99 ("condizioni," p. 106).
[5] p. 312 ("armenti," p. 316).
[6] p. 43 ("Alcuni si diletteranno più della modestia; alcun' altri d'un omo attivo ed inquieto," p. 51).
[7] p. 77.　　　[8] p. 84.　　　[9] p. 70.　　　[10] p. 78.
[11] p. 124 ("Non usarà il nostro Cortegiano prosonzion sciocca; non sarà apportator di nove fastidiose . . . non sarà cianciatore," p. 130).

"Yet will we not have him for al that so lustie to make braverie in woordes, and to bragge that he hathe wedded his harneys for his wife" [1] cannot be surpassed for vigor; nor can "Let us leave these blinde busardes in their owne erroure" [2] as a rendering of the plain "Lassamo questi ciechi nel lor errore." [3] His images also are most striking: the courtier is not to carry his head "so like a malthorse for feare of ruffling his haire." [4] Thus Hoby's determination to use native turns of speech often stands him in good stead, and his pages are filled with words that were destined to become the general stock in trade of the Elizabethan dramatists. To have "a faint heart"; [5] to be "a mocking stocke to the verye chil-dren"; [6] Fortune burying "in the botomles depth the most worthy to be exalted"; [7] the constant use of "stomake" as a translation for both "animo" and "core," "but with a boulde stomake despising her stormes" [8] — all these suggest the speech of the theater.

Another characteristic of his style that was to be one of the principal characteristics of Elizabethan prose is the introduction of a verb of action whenever possible.

[1] p. 49 ("Il quale non volemo però che si mostri tanto fiero, che sempre stia in su le brave parole, e dica aver tolto la corazza per moglie," p. 57).

[2] p. 86.

[3] p. 93.

[4] p. 60 ("così fermo per paura di non guastarsi la zazzera," p. 68).

[5] p. 53 ("estrema viltà," p. 61).

[6] p. 53 ("la baia da fanciulli," p. 61).

[7] p. 46 ("nell' abisso i più degni d'esser esaltati," p. 54).

[8] p. 31 ("anzi, sprezzando con l'animo valoroso le procelle di quella," p. 38).

The recommendation that the courtier should not be too often in the eyes of the multitude, for "contynuance *goeth nyghe to geve* a manne hys fyll," [1] where Castiglione had written simply that "la assiduità sazia molto"; [2] the statement of the distinction conferred by the desire "to *wade in* everye thyng a little farther then other menne"; [3] and "matters that *taste* somewhat of jugglers crafte" [1] for "hanno del giocolare" [2] — all these reveal the Englishman's instinctive effort for the stronger, more picturesque expression. Such verbs are the greatest single factor in giving energy to his words, as when he writes "goe against the shotte of a Cannon" [4] where the Italian verb is "aspettar," [5] "fell to daunsinge" [6] for "cominciarono a danzare," [7] "to roote that oute of your mind" [8] for "per levar dall' animo." [9] One of the most vivid instances of all is to be seen where the fault of Fra Serafino is said to be that "he cannot kepe his handes from the table, especially as long as there is any meat *styrryng*." [10]

The result of Hoby's robust manner and his Saxon verbs and epithets is that his book does not have a literary finish to remove it from everyday speech. There is a vast difference both in sound and implication between "Il nostro Cortegiano non debba far profession

---

[1] p. 55. [2] p. 63. [3] p. 54 ("di passar, etc.," p. 61).
[4] p. 53. [5] p. 61. [6] p. 295.
[7] p. 299. [8] p. 296. [9] p. 300.
[10] p. 61 ("Non saper levar le mani dalla tavola, almen fin che in tutto non ne sono levate ancora le vivande," p. 69).

d'esser gran mangiatore, nè bevitore"[1] and "Oure Courtier ought not to professe to be a glutton nor a dronkard."[2] It is even greater between "rude and boysterous beehaviours that smell of the plough and cart a thousand mile of"[2] and "certi modo da contadino, che chiamano la zappa e l'aratro mille miglia di lontano."[3] When Hoby wants to express his opinion of certain people, he does not call them "sciocchi" or "foolish," but "untowardly asseheades,"[4] and does not remark that they "excite one to disgust," but that "they move a manne to vomite."[5] No more does he say "Vattene in malora,"[6] or "To perdition with you,"[7] but "Get thee hence in the Dyvelles name."[8]

The use of this blunt English carries force in such expressions as "fell starke dead to the grounde."[9] It is in keeping with the temper of the passage where poor Italy is described as "a prey and bootie in the teeth of straunge nations."[10] But too much vigor is apparent when "lothesomenesse" becomes Hoby's habitual translation for "fastidio"; and it is fantastic when "il mormorar suave d'un vivo fonte"[11] is metamorphosed into "the sweete roaringe of a plentifull and livelye springe."[12] What is more serious, the sense of passages of a philo-

---

[1] p. 153.   [2] p. 148.   [3] p. 154.
[4] p. 41.   [5] p. 141.   [6] p. 192.
[7] The rendering in Opdycke's modern version, p. 150.
[8] p. 185.
[9] p. 238 ("cadde morta in terra," p. 243).
[10] p. 324 ("preda esposta a genti strane," p. 329).
[11] p. 161.   [12] p. 155.

sophic tenor is altogether altered. For instance, to say
that if a person does not care for music "a manne may
assuredly thinke him not to be well in his wittes," [1] does
not convey at all Castiglione's meaning that "his spirit
is not well attuned." [2]

Where Hoby excels is in the colloquial tone of his
book. His journal had already testified to his ability to
write a lively idiom, as for instance, on his first diplomatic mission to France, the account that:

> At Chasteubriant the French King shewed my Lord Mar-
> quess great plesure and disport, sometime in plaing at tenice,
> sometime in shooting, sometime in hunting the bore, some-
> time at the palla malla, and sometime with his great boisterlie
> Britons wrastling with my lorde's yemen of Cornwall, who
> had much a do to gete the upper hand of them: and everie
> night ther was dansing in the great hall, and somtime musike
> in the King's Privie Chamber.[3]

The same racy qualities mark his translation. When it is
said that the magnetism of the duchess' personality
"made men to her becke," [4] we have traveled far from
the courtly atmosphere of Urbino where "she seemed to
attune us all to her own quality and tone." [5] "The
which being agreed upon of all handes" [6] for "così con-

---

p. 90.

The Italian text is "si po tener certo che abbia gli spiriti discordanti
l'un dall' altro," p. 97.

[3] *A Booke of the Travaile and Lief of Me*, p. 72.

[4] p. 33.

[5] Opdycke's translation, p. 11, of "parea che tutti alla qualità e forma
di lei temperasse," p. 40.

[6] p. 100.

fermando ognuno," [1] "gesse you" [2] for "imaginate," [3]
"to square one wyth an other" [4] for "dissentir," [5] and
"to come into a greater pecke of troubles" [6] for "peggio
ve n'avverrà," [7] all indicate a similar quality. The
courtier has become an Englishman, but he is less the
scholar, and more the man of action. Descriptive richness has been substituted in his speech for philosophic
dignity, and when he comes to discuss Platonic love, he
must fit it into his own terms, and speak of "a smacke of
the right blisse" [8] instead of "dà gusto di vera beati-
tudine." [9]

This being the case, Hoby's greatest success naturally
lies in the crispness and ease of his dialogues. He falls
instinctively into the right conversational phrases: "Goo
to, saye on then"; [10] "Therfore sticke not (Count) to pay
this debt"; [11] "Behoulde I beseeche ye, saide then the
Dutchesse"; [12] "Marke me the Lorde Hippolitus"; [13]
"Truely a man would weene." [14] These phrases have a
freedom not suggested by the Italian, and are never far
from the cadence of the Elizabethan stage. The vividness that Hoby achieves reveals how fully he was caught

[1] p. 107.   [2] p. 211.   [3] p. 215.   [4] p. 288.
[5] p. 294.   [6] p. 228.   [7] p. 233.
[8] p. 362. See also the account of "the right aungelike beawtie," p. 35, above.
[9] p. 368.
[10] p. 342 ("Or dite adunque," p. 347).
[11] p. 99 ("Però non rifiutate, Conte, di pagar questo debito," p. 106).
[12] p. 56 ("Vedete, disse allora la signora Duchessa," p. 63).
[13] p. 45 ("E per darvi un esempio: vedete il signor don Ippolito," p. 53).
[14] p. 59 ("Che di certo pare," p. 67).

by the force of the book. Sometimes it also hints that he is stating his own views on a question. Certainly "trifling tales"[1] is the scornful name his distinguished contemporaries fastened upon the "novelle."[2] And it is in keeping with the nature of the serious humanist to term the efforts of a woman to beautify herself not "fastidii"[3] but "lothesomenesse";[4] and to speak not of the faults, but of the "curst prankes,"[5] of youth. Also, in general, Hoby pours more blood into his adjectives than Castiglione: he emphasizes the "*greedye* desire"[6] of sex where the Italian wrote the single word "appetito,"[7] and "this *rotten* life that lasteth twoo dayes,"[8] where the original adjective is "caduca"[9] or "frail." So it may be more than chance when he reverses this tendency and in several instances tones down the words "divino" and "divinamente." It may indicate his stern Protestant spirit that will not let the attributes of God be applied to the works of man, and therefore causes him to say, not that the ancients were godlike, but that they were "of most perfection in every vertue";[10] and to decree that the courtier should know Greek, not because of the many things "in quella divinamente scritte sono,"[11] but because of their being written "with greate excellencye."[12] But it is dangerous business to try to discover

---

[1] p. 37.   [2] p. 45.   [3] p. 87.
[4] p. 79.   [5] p. 121.   [6] p. 306.
[7] p. 311.   [8] p. 84.   [9] p. 91.
[10] p. 108 ("veramente divini in ogni virtù," p. 114).
[11] p. 92.   [12] p. 85.

the personality of a translator, and if the words just
mentioned are to be cited as showing Hoby's views and
interests, so must be his additions to the following passage: "Have ye not hadde an *eye* otherwhyle, whan
eyther in the stretes goynge to Churche, or in anye other
place, or in sportyng, or by any chaunce it happeneth
that a woman lyfteth up her clothes so *high*, that she
sheweth her foote, and sometime a litle of her *pretye*
legge unwittinglye." [1] And a little farther on he mentions "her hose sittynge cleane to her legge" when Castiglione had merely written "calze polite."

Where Hoby fails is in those passages that demanded
a familiarity in dealing with abstract terms. The proper
words do not come readily to his hand. "Cortegiana," a
word of supreme importance in the treatise, is variously
rendered by "Courtiers' trade," "Courtlinesse," "Cour-
tiership," and "Courting." "Contemplazioni" [2] is not
suggested by "behouldinges," [3] nor "imitazioni" [4] by
"followinge." [5] A philosophical vocabulary was essential, and this Hoby did not possess. He always translates "costumi," [6] not as "customs," but "condicions";[7]

---

[1] p. 81 ("Avete voi posto cura talor, quando, o per le strade andando alle
chiese o ad altro loco, e giocando o per altra causa, accade che una donna
tanto della robba si leva, che il piede e spesso un poco di gambetta senza pensarvi mostra," p. 88).

[2] p. 369.

[3] Women's souls are not "accustomed in behouldinges," p. 364.

[4] p. 73.

[5] "Take dylygente heede to folowinge, without the whiche I judge no
man canne wryte well," p. 66.

[6] p. 89.   [7] p. 82.

"prosunzione" [1] as "malapertnesse"; [2] and "sprezza-
tura" [3] — one of the key-words of the book, since it de-
notes the manner of the courtier, without which all his
accomplishments go for naught — is rendered, not very
happily, as "reckelesnes." [4] And finally, "magnani-
mità," [5] the crown of the whole Aristotelian structure
of virtues, is hardly recognizable in "stoutnesse of
courage." [6]

Again and again the words of Hoby's *Courtier* reveal
the vast difference between Italy and England in the
mid-sixteenth century. The constant use of "carpen-
ters" [5] for "architetti," [7] and "carvinge" [8] for "scul-
tura," [9] is the expression of an uncultivated society.
The fine arts of the Renaissance had not yet taken root
on English soil. The statement that the painter can
"discover unto you also in the outward sight of an upright wal the plainnesse and farnesse, more and lesse, as
pleaseth him," [10] does not seem to present an adequate
basis for the appreciation of the relative merits of Leo-
nardo, Mantegna, and Raphael. The word for "cultivated" is once left out, [11] and at other times is weakened

---

[1] p. 134.   [2] p. 128.   [3] p. 67.

[4] p. 59. There is no exact equivalent in English, but "negligence" or
"nonchalance" comes closer to it than Hoby's rendering.

[5] p. 314.   [6] p. 310.   [7] p. 319.

[8] p. 247.   [9] p. 253.

[10] p. 94. Here the sense of the original is that "he shows the foreground
and distance all on a single surface."

[11] "In that first rude age," p. 68, for "in quella prima età rozza ed inculta," p. 76.

into some such expression as, "The mind is muche more
worthye then the bodye, so deserveth it also to bee
better decked and polished." [1] Or again, when the courtier is recommended to bestow great diligence on making
his writing "più culta," [2] the sense of "refined" is
scarcely conveyed by "more trimme." [3] Hoby was incapable of translating Castiglione's refinement, for English society had not yet achieved the development of the
Italian.

No one would assert his *Courtier* to be great prose, but
its qualities foretell the approach of Sir Thomas North
and Shakespeare. If it does not possess the dignity of
the original, there is rich compensation in its pictur-
esqueness. [4] And often Hoby's power of close description,
which had made the account of his travels so vivid, en-
ables him to add specific detail that is the very essence
of the dramatic. For instance, near the close, where
Castiglione wrote "Quando già erano per uscir dalla
camera," [5] and the literal modern version is "As they
were about to quit the room," [6] Hoby gives it, "As they

[1] p. 81 ("più culto e più ornato," p. 88).
[2] p. 71.   [3] p. 64.
[4] For example, "I knowe not then how it will stande wel, in steade of en-
riching this tunge, and of gevyng it majestye and light, to make it poore,
sclender, bare and dark, and to seeke to shut it up into so narrowe a rowme,
that everye man should be compelled to folow onely Petrarca and Boccaccio," p. 76. Such an expression as "to shut it up into so narrowe a rowme"
for the unadorned "di metterla in tante angustie," p. 84, is doubtless out of
keeping with the spirit of a learned discussion of language. But it has a savor
of its own.
[5] p. 371.   [6] Opdycke, p. 309.

were now passing out at the great chambre doore," [1] and
the scene itself is living before our eyes.

In passages where the dramatic elements are most
strongly implied, Hoby's work is really magnificent.
Take, for instance, that moment in the first night when
the interest of the discussion was at its very height:

> And then was there heard a great scraping of feet in the
> floore with a cherme of loude speaking, and upon that every
> man tourninge him selfe about, saw at the Chambre doore
> appeare a light of torches, and by and by after entred in the
> L. Generall with a greate and noble traine.[2]

Here the variations from the Italian are extremely
slight, yet it is hard for the reader to believe that such a
striking description can be a translation. The same is
true of the passage on the dawn where Castiglione's style
had attained its most beautiful level. Bembo had completed his oration on love, when all of a sudden the company was amazed to find that light had already begun
to creep in between the clefts of the windows. They
threw open the casements, and

> saw alredie risen in the East a faire morninge like unto the
> coulour of roses, and all sterres voided, savinge onelye the
> sweete Governesse of the heaven, Venus, whiche keapeth the
> boundes of the nyght and the day, from whiche appeered to
> blowe a sweete blast, that filling the aer with a bytinge cold,
> begane to quicken the tunable notes of the prety birdes,
> emong the hushing woodes of the hilles at hande. Whereupon
> they all, takinge their leave with reverence of the Dutchesse,
> departed toward their lodginges without torche, the light of
> the day sufficing.[3]

[1] p. 365.   [2] p. 97.   [3] p. 365.

V

Hoby wrote with many limitations, but also with an immediacy to his subject that has not been within the power of the later translators of the book. Interest in *The Courtier*, waning with the disappearance of the generation of Elizabethan courtiers, was revived in the eighteenth century. Johnson told Boswell: "The best book that ever was written upon good breeding, *Il Cortegiano*, by Castiglione, grew up at the little Court of Urbino, and you should read it." [1] But how little Johnson understood its spirit is manifest from his declaration that its object was "to teach the minuter decencies and inferiour duties, to regulate the practice of daily conversation, to correct those depravities which are rather ridiculous than criminal, and remove those grievances which, if they produce no lasting calamities, impress hourly vexation." [2] The ideal courtier was no longer Sidney or Raleigh but the Earl of Chesterfield; the scholar-gentleman had degenerated into the man of fashion. And the two eighteenth-century translations of Castiglione are as far from the tone of the original. [3]

[1] *The Journal of a Tour to the Hebrides*, ed. Birbeck Hill (London, 1887), p. 276.

[2] Johnson, *Works* (Oxford, 1825), VII, 428. This passage in the Life of Addison is applied to both Della Casa and Castiglione. It is true of *Galateo* (1558, translated into English in 1576), which is a manual on good manners, but not of *Il Cortegiano*.

[3] After a lapse of a hundred years, Clerke's Latin version was reprinted (with revisions) at Cambridge in 1713. The two English translations are by

Other limitations are found in the twentieth-century translation. Where Hoby declares that the man who larded his talk with archaisms would be "a laughing stock," [1] the version of 1901 says "besides exciting ridicule." [2] The supposedly refined taste that substitutes "impudicity" [3] for "wantonnesse" [4] is incapable of making the book seem very fresh. This is evident not only in the more colloquial passages, [5] as can be observed by setting this beside the version from Hoby:

They saw that a beautiful dawn of rosy hue was already born in the east, and that all the stars had vanished save Venus, sweet mistress of the sky, who holds the bonds of night and day; from which there seemed to breathe a gentle wind that filled the air with crisp coolness and began to waken sweet choruses of joyous birds in the murmuring forests of the hills hard by. So, having reverently taken leave of my lady Duchess, they all started towards their chambers without light of torches, that of day being enough for them. [6]

Robert Samber, 1724 (second edition, 1729), and A. P. Castiglione, Gent., who claimed to be of the same family as the author, 1727 (second edition, 1737). Raleigh characterizes them thus: "Castiglione's translation is dull and flat, Samber's is dull and pert," p. lxi.

[1] p. 63. The 1727 translation says that "he would make himself both ridiculous and tedious." A. P. Castiglione, *The Courtier* (London, 1727), p. 52.

[2] Opdycke, p. 39.

[3] *Ibid.*, p. 208.

[4] p. 249.

[5] Contrast the robust swing of "As a man of the Countrye caryinge a coffer upon his shoulders, chaunced therwithall to give Cato a harde pushe, and afterward said: 'Give roume'" (Hoby, p. 184), with "As where a rustic, who was carrying a box on his shoulders, jostled it against Cato, and then said, 'Have a care'" (Opdycke, p. 149).

[6] Opdycke, p. 309.

"A beautiful dawn of rosy hue" instead of "a faire morninge like unto the coulour of roses"—the magic of the words is gone. The twentieth-century translation is the work of a scholar. It is accurate; it is furnished with valuable notes; the volume suggests the life of the Court of Urbino by reproducing the Raphael and Titian portraits of the leading characters in the book. But the writing is without distinction; smoothly, carefully, it reproduces a dead classic. The aristocratic, many-sided courtier is as remote from the Court of St. James's as he is from our White House. He was the dominant figure in society only in that brief span when the medieval had not yet been wholly absorbed by the Renaissance, and the feudal order had not been superseded by the system of parliaments. No modern gentleman has the range of his accomplishments; rarely in our rigid specialization does the man of action possess the fullness of his culture. If the reader of English wants to feel his power and charm, he must seek it in the pages of one for whom the ideal of the courtier was a living symbol, in those of the man whom Queen Elizabeth created Sir Thomas Hoby.

CHAPTER III

North's Plutarch
(1579)

I

PLUTARCH "is so universall and so full," said Montaigne in the English of John Florio, "that upon all occasions, and whatsoever extravagant subject you have undertaken, he intrudeth himselfe into your work, and gently reacheth you a helpe-affording hand, fraught with rare embelishments, and inexhaustible of precious riches. . . . He can no sooner come in my sight, or if I cast but a glance upon him, but I pull some legge or wing from him." [1] And again, Plutarch "of all the authors I know hath best commixt arte with nature, and coupled judgement with learning." [2]

These remarks express the attitude that became universal in England during Elizabeth's reign. Plutarch grew to be as widely read as any author of classical antiquity, and his influence was enormous. His name had not appeared among the authors prescribed by Thomas Elyot as essential for the education of a good Governour (1531), nor in the list of books cited by Ascham as

[1] Montaigne, *Essays*, Tudor Translations (London, 1893), III, 102–103.
[2] III, 129.

held most valuable by the worthy Master Cheke.[1] But Ascham himself called in Plutarch to defend the argument in *Toxophilus* (1545), and his popularity with the general reader had begun ten years before, though in an indirect fashion. In 1535 Lord Berners had issued his translation of Guevara's *Golden Boke of Marcus Aurelius*, many of the best anecdotes and illustrations of which are taken from the Greek moralist. Guevara's vogue was instantaneous and prolonged. Berners' translation had reached its seventh edition by 1557, when Thomas North published *The Diall of Princes*, a fuller version of the same book. Both continued to be reprinted throughout the century, and, although their supposed influence on Lyly's style has been greatly exaggerated, *Euphues* shows the same moral and discursive cast as *The Diall* and may well have been encouraged by Guevara's popularity. Lyly is also more directly indebted to Plutarch, especially in the discussion of education between Euphues and Ephoebus, although he probably modeled this, not on the *Morals*, but on Erasmus' *Colloquies*.

By the end of the century the mark of Plutarch on English literature had become far more pronounced.

---

[1] "Yea, I have heard worthie M. Cheke many times say: I would have a good student passe and iorney through all Authors both Greke and Latin: but he that will dwell in these few bookes onelie: first, in Gods holie Bible, and then ioyne with it, Tullie in Latin, Plato, Aristotle: Zenophon: Isocrates: and Demosthenes in Greke: must needes prove an excellent man."—*The Scholemaster*, p. 129.

Bacon cites him frequently. The mind of Sir William Cornwallis, to name a characteristic English gentleman, seems to have been molded by his breadth and nobility. Burton's *Anatomy* is packed with references to Xylander's Latin version of the *Morals*; and the way in which Plutarch's thought and stories constantly flow into the pages of Jeremy Taylor reveals what an essential part of English humanism he had then become. But he had caught the popular imagination much earlier through a series of plays. Robert Garnier's *Marc Antoine*, as translated by Sidney's sister, the Countess of Pembroke, in 1590, drew the attention of Elizabethan dramatists to Plutarchan themes. Samuel Daniel wrote his *Cleopatra* (1594) confessedly in the desire to provide a companion piece to the *Antonie* of his patroness. Kyd translated another of Garnier's dramas in *Pompey the Great, his faire Cornelia's Tragedie* (1595). Fulke Greville attempted a play on "the irregular passions" of Antonie and Cleopatra, who "forsook empire to follow sensuality," but burnt it, fearing that an unfortunate analogy might be suggested to Essex and the Queen. The Scotchman William Alexander issued, in 1607, *The Monarchicke Tragedies*, including closet dramas on Alexander and Julius Caesar. Beaumont and Fletcher's *False One* (c. 1619), which deals with the stay of Cæsar in Egypt, is also indebted to Plutarch. But the popular culmination had been reached in the three Roman tragedies of Shakespeare.

The reason for this greatly increased vogue of Plutarch is also expressed by Montaigne. He himself had "no skille of the Greeke," and consequently, when one of his countrymen produced magnificent translations of both the *Lives* and the *Morals*, he wrote:

I do with some reason, as me seemeth, give pricke and praise unto Jaques Amiot above all our French writers, not only for his natural purity, and pure elegancie of the tongue, wherein he excelleth all others, nor for his indefatigable constancie of so long and toyle-some a labour, nor for the unsearchable depth of his knowledge, having so successefully-happy been able to explaine an Author so close and thorny, and unfold a writer so mysterious and entangled . . . but above all I kon him thanks that he hath had the hap to chuse, and knowledge to cull-out so worthy a worke, and a booke so fit to the purpose, therewith to make so unvaluable a present unto his Countrie. We that are in the number of the ignorant had beene utterly confounded, had not his booke raised us from out the dust of ignorance: God-a-mercy his endevours we dare now both speake and write: Even Ladies are therewith able to confront Masters of arts: "It is our breviarie." [1]

It was Plutarch's good fortune to find a translator like Amyot, who reproduced him so vividly that he became the breviary of one of the two greatest writers in sixteenth-century France. And without Amyot, Sir Thomas North could not have written—North, whose words stirred Shakespeare's imagination more deeply than it was stirred by those of any other man, save possibly Marlowe. Bishop Amyot was a scholar who was capable not only of tireless work with the various edi-

[1] II, 41.

tions and manuscripts, but also of writing a rare style. As a result, his influence reigned supreme on the work which, after Malory's *Morte D'Arthur* and the *Book of Common Prayer*, is the earliest great masterpiece of English prose. North was well acquainted with French, Spanish, and Italian, but seems to have had little Greek. Consequently, the merits of his Plutarch can be judged only in relation to Amyot's.

II

But first it is well to know something of the character and attainments of this man who was to dedicate his great *Lives of the Noble Grecians and Romans* to Queen Elizabeth. Few enough facts concerning him have been preserved. Born about 1535, Thomas North was the younger son of Edward, first Baron North. His father was a man of law and a gifted politician who managed to stay in high favor during the swift changes of the reigns of Henry VII, Henry VIII, Edward VI, and Jane, whom he supported, and yet secured pardon from Mary, and again from Elizabeth. Thomas was probably educated at Peterhouse, Cambridge, and, at the age of twenty-two, he was entered in the family profession at Lincoln's Inn. But in the same year he showed his own true bent by translating Guevara's *Diall of Princes*, "ryght necessary and pleasaunt to all Gentylmen and others whiche are lovers of virtue." This version was avowedly made from the French, but a remark in the second edition that certain appended letters were "not written in the French tongue," reveals the fact that North was also able to cope with the original. This evidence of a command of languages was increased in 1570, when he translated *The Morall Philosophie of Doni* from the Italian, and suggests that the young man must have spent his early years in much the same fashion as Hoby.

But the only existing record of his travels is of the journey that he made in 1574 in the retinue of his brother Roger, the second baron, on an embassy to the Court of Henry III. A visit to France at this time was of the greatest significance for the translator, since Amyot had completed his long undertaking of *Les Vies de Plutarque* in 1559, and his *Œuvres Morales* in 1572. After having been tutor to the princes Charles IX and Henry III, he had received the appointment of Grand Almoner of France, and had become Bishop of Auxerre four years before North's appearance at the French court. With their similarity of interests it seems inevitable that the two would have met. At all events, North was doubtless reading Amyot's *Vies* by this time, since his own translation appeared only five years later.

North lived for more than twenty years after the appearance of his Plutarch, and prepared a second and a third edition for the press, but he does not seem to have engaged in any new work. He had settled in Cambridge, where the freedom of the city had been conferred upon him in 1568. His brother gave him "a lease of a house

and household stuff" in 1576, but, in spite of this gift
and the provision that had been made for him in his
father's will, he seems to have been always in need. The
year after the appearance of his famous translation,
Leicester wrote recommending him to Burghley, and
declared him to be "a very honest gentleman, and hath
many good things in him, which are drowned only by
poverty." He was twice married, and at least two children, a son and a daughter, are known to have reached
maturity. His grandnephew Dudley, the fourth baron,
described Thomas North as "a man of courage," who,
at the time of the Armada, had taken command of three
hundred men of Ely. He was knighted three years after
this event, and subsequently served on the county Com-
mission of Peace. In 1598 he received a grant of £20
from Cambridge, and in 1601 a pension of £40 from the
Queen. The third edition of the *Lives* came out in 1603,
but it is thought that he had died before that year.

An important fact to be recognized before dealing
with North's masterpiece is that this country gentleman
was not a man of one book. It is the Plutarch by which
he is remembered to-day, but both his early works present a distinguished style. They were both widely read
by his contemporaries, *The Morall Philosophie of Doni*
going through two editions, and *The Diall of Princes*
reaching its fourth by 1619.[1] Furthermore, the manner

---

[1] *The Diall of Princes* appeared in 1557, was reprinted "with an amplifi-
cation also of a fourth booke entituled *The Favored Courtier*" in 1568, 1582,
and 1619. *The Morall Philosophie of Doni* was issued in 1570 and 1601.

in which each book is written is quite distinct. Unlike
Holland, North did not remake all his authors in the
same image. Under his hand they all became Englishmen, to be sure; yet each maintained an individuality of
his own.

The three works are very different, but the translator's purpose is substantially the same in each. In
offering to Queen Mary the firstfruits of his "small
knowledge and tender years," his version of Guevara's
popular book, his belief is that

there is no Auctor (the sacred letters set aparte) that more
effectuously setteth out the omnipotencie of God, the frailty
of men, the inconstancie of Fortune, the vanity of this worlde,
the miserie of this life, and finally that more plainely teacheth
the good whiche mortal men ought to pursue, and the evil
that al men ought to flye; then this present worke doth. The
whiche is so ful of highe doctrine, so adourned with auncient
histories, so auctorised with grave sentences, and so beautified with apte simylitudes; that I knowe not whose eyes in
redynge it can be weried, nor whose eares in hearinge it not
satisfied.[1]

The Diall of Princes is a formless series of dissertations
with copious anecdotes drawn from nearly all the classic
historians of Greece and Rome. But throughout its end-
less didactic discussion of a mother's duty to her children, the use of wine, and the proper relation of the

[1] Dedication to "The Mooste hyghe and vertuouse Princesse Mary" of
The Diall of Princes, Compiled by the reverende father in God, Don Anthony
of Guevara, Bysshop of Guadix, Preacher and Cronicler to Charles the fyft
Emperour of Rome, Englysshed oute of the Frenche, by Thomas North,
second sonne of the Lorde North, 1557.

sexes, the ground of its appeal to North is plain.[1] Its first book "entreateth what excellencie is in the Prince, that is a good Christian; and contrary-wise, what evils do followe him that is a cruel tyrant." The whole is a plea for moderation in politics and behavior. With the cardinal assumption that the Prince is the fountainhead of all moral excellence as well as the soul of honor, it emphasizes the need of orderly government, and — although Guevara was an inquisitor — of religious toleration. Any serious-minded Englishman in the middle of the sixteenth century could not fail to perceive how much good such a book as this would do for his disordered country.

The prose of the translation shows an extraordinary finish for a young man of twenty-two who was writing at a time when the state of the English language was as uncertain as Tudor politics. North's words flow steadily in a developed rhythmical pattern, of which the passage from the dedication serves as a fair example. But that, as befitting an address to royalty, shows the translator in his most elaborate vein. His ordinary style is more subdued,[2] and although his balanced sentences some-

[1] I am indebted here to K. N. Colvile's essay on Sir Thomas North in *Fame's Twilight* (London, 1923).

[2] An instance from the story (taken out of Plutarch) of Sinatus and Sinoris: "Though *Camma* was now maryed and that shee was in the protection of the goddesse Diana: yet notwithstanding her olde friend *Sinoris* died for her sake, and by all means possible he served her, continually he importuned her, dayly he followed her, and hourely he required her. And all this he did, upon certaine hope he had, that such diligent service should suffice to

times run thin and tedious, this artificial quality is simply the descendant of medieval rhetoric and is never carried to the extreme of the devices and conceits of Euphues.[1]

Thirteen years later, when North made his second translation,[2] his choice was again dominated by civic purpose. He gave to his countrymen one of the most charming books of beast fables ever written;[3] but what was doubtless uppermost in his mind was its moral philosophy, and the hope that by its means his readers might "blotte out many malignant effects of this (alas)

make her change her sacred minde: and as she had chosen *Sinatus* for her husbande openly, so hee thought she should take him for her friende secretly. For many women are as men without tast through sicknes, the which eate more of that that is hurtfull and forbidden: then of that which is healthsome, and commanded." — Ed. 1619, p. 190.

[1] The theory that Lyly owed his style to Guevara through the medium of North, which was developed by F. Landmann, *Der Euphuismus* (Giessen, 1881), has now been generally discarded. See especially M. W. Croll's introduction to his edition of *Euphues* (New York, 1916).

[2] *The Morall Philosophie of Doni:* Drawne out of the auncient writers. A worke first compiled in the Indian tongue, and afterwards reduced into divers other languages: and now lastly Englished out of Italian by Thomas North, Brother to the Right Honorable Sir Roger North, Knight, Lorde North of Kyrtheling, 1570.

[3] North says that it was "first compiled in the Indian tongue, and afterwardes transferred into divers and sundrie other languages: as the Persian, Arabian, Hebrue, Latine, Spanish, and Italian: and now reduced into our vulgar speeche." J. Jacobs, who republished North's translation under the title of *The Earliest English Version of The Fables of Bidpai* (London, 1888), concluded that it was "the English version of an Italian adaptation of a Spanish translation of a Latin version of a Hebrew translation of an Arabic adaptation of the Pehlevi version of the Indian original."—Introduction, p. xi. Doni is simply the name of the Italian translator.

our crooked age." [1] But that hope did not prevent him from relishing the delightful qualities of these stories of the bull and the mule and the fox, or from bringing them out to the full with a command of prose astonishing in its variety. His humorous touch is delightful, as in the description of "the poore Lowse that was no great horse to leap," [2] or in the story of three fishes, one of whom was "a certaine let me alone, and drowsie fishe," who "was called of the Frogge ten times that hee shoulde rise and awake: Whooe, but all in vayne." [3] His pages are full of the richest slang the English language has ever known. He knows how to write extremely racy speeches, introduced by such realistic phrases as "Tut a figge!" or "What the goodyere!" The frog punched the fish "for the nonste, and iogged him agayne to make him awake, but it would not be. And he, tut lyke a sluggarde, aunswered him, I will ryse anone, anone." [3] North's vigor is amazing: "His Moyleship [Muleship] bravely yerked out with both legges, and lively shook his eares and head. He brayed and flong as he had bene madde." [4] But no less amazing is his ability to sound the restrained music of such a sentence as, "Sure this worldly life representeth no more but the little worlde of our bodie, which carrieth a wonderfull presence: and that little breath of ours once spent, it is then but a shadowe, dust and smoke." [5] And "To be alone it

---

[1] p. 14. [2] p. 140. [3] p. 134.
[4] p. 96. [5] p. 46.

griveth us: to be accompanied it troubleth us: to live long it werieth us: and sufficient contenteth us not"[1] bears a cadence that would grace the finest book of devotions.

III

A man who could write with such a range of style was a very great master of prose. And when he came to his chief work, he had, in addition, the good fortune to translate from an admirable model. Amyot had undertaken Plutarch's *Lives* with the firm belief "that the office of a fit translator consisteth not onely in the faithfull expressing of his authors meaning, but also in a certaine resembling and shadowing out of the forme of his style and the manner of his speaking."[2] But he perceived the gulf that lay between himself and Plutarch. He knew that the temper of his French was remote from that of the somewhat harsh and crabbed late Greek. And he was determined to write his own language, not rack it, to use those words — and the principle is admirable — "qui nous sembleront plus doux, qui sonneront le mieux à l'oreille, qui seront coutumièrement en la bouche des bien parlants, qui seront bons françois et non etrangers." Amyot also knew how far his countrymen were from an intimate knowledge of classical customs and history.

---

[1] p. 31.

[2] "Amiot to the Readers," translated by North, *Plutarch*, Tudor Translations, ed. G. Wyndham (London, 1895), I, 24. All page references are to this edition.

His desire was really to translate, to bear this "Treasorie of all rare and perfect learning" across the ages into his own land. Consequently, although he wrote no word that was not calculated to reveal his author's meaning, he added and explained where the situation seemed to demand it.

But throughout, his translation is extremely close. His additions are few, and chiefly for the purpose of making his meaning more compact.[1] His effort centered in the desire for precision and clarity, and when Plutarch had written οἱ Λακεδαιμόνιοι, he felt that the sense demanded elaboration to "les Lacedaemoniens qui tenoient les pas des montaignes."[2] He explained historical allusions: Ὄναβις is called "le tyrant Onabis";[3] πυλάδην τὸν κιθαρῳδὸν ᾄδοντα τοὺς Τιμοθέου Πέρσας is rendered as "le musicien Pylades qui chantoit sus son luc *ung certain poeme* du poete Thimoteus, *lequel se nomme* les Perses."[4] Amyot seemed instinctively to describe Greek customs in a way that would make them fully comprehensible to his contemporaries. He wrote of the pagan religion in terms of the Christian, of "devotes ceremonies" and "sainctz cantiques." Ἡγεμονίαν is modernized into "une

---

[1] An excellent study of Amyot's translation has been made by René Sturel, *Jacques Amyot, Traducteur des Vies Parallèles de Plutarque* (Paris, 1908). Especially valuable are pp. 187–267, which analyze Amyot's method of handling the Greek.

[2] Sturel, p. 210. All the following examples were taken by him from Amyot's manuscript of the life of Philopoemen.

[3] p. 219.

[4] p. 221.

compagnie de gens d'armes," [1] and ἵππαρχος into "capitaine general de la gendarmerie." [2]

The most common addition is Amyot's use of a doublet for a single word. Sometimes this is designed to give greater scope to the meaning, as when μέγαν στρατηγόν is translated "ung sage et vaillant capitaine." [3] Or a learned word is familiarized by being joined with a popular word: "les grands proffictz et emolumens" [4] for τῶν ὠφελείων. Very often, however, the doublets seem to be used not to satisfy any demand of the meaning, but for the sound and pattern of the prose. Such are "fut arse et bruslée," [4] or the tripled noun in "car ce n'estoit pas petit accroissement de dignité, puissance, et authorité" [5] for the simple οὐ γὰρ ἦν μικρόν.

Although this is not a study of Amyot's translation, a brief suggestion of his methods is indispensable in accounting for some of the qualities in North. For it is clear that Amyot's imagination and skill had already brought Plutarch into the sixteenth century. Even his language shows qualities that we are accustomed to think of as essentially Elizabethan. The importance of Amyot for North was of the same magnitude as that of the earlier versions of the Bible for the translators of the King James version. Amyot gave him a definite support to lean on, relieved him from the tortuous necessity of working out the meaning, and allowed him to devote the bulk of his attention to the development of his style. As a result, North's words stalk with a majesty and sureness unrivaled in any other sixteenth-century English book. And the whole further course of English prose owes a greater debt to the Bishop of Auxerre than has ever been generally recognized.[1]

IV

North acknowledged his obligations by writing large on his title-page that the *Lives* had been first "translated out of Greeke into French by James Amyot," and then "out of French into Englishe" by himself. He was at one with the Frenchman in his enthusiasm for Plutarch. He reprinted Amyot's "Epistle to the Reader," which sufficiently declares "the profit of stories, and the prayse of the Author." [2] Amyot had said of the work that "C'est en somme un recueil abbregé de tout ce qui a esté de plus memorable & de plus digne faict ou dict par les plus grands roys, plus excellens capitaines & plus sages hommes des deux plus nobles, plus vertueuses & plus puissantes nations qui jamais furent au monde." [3] North adopted the same tone in his dedication to Eliza-

---

[1] Attention has been drawn to this point by S. Lee in *The French Renaissance in England* (New York, 1910), to which book I am indebted in this chapter.

[2] North, "To the Reader," I, 7.

[3] Amyot, in his dedication to Henry II (which naturally is not included by North), *Les Vies des Hommes Illustres de Plutarque* (Paris, 1783–1786), I, xiv. All page references are to this edition.

beth, and further emphasized the strong effect which the
lives of such heroes might have upon England's national
life. For

well may the Readers thinke, if they have done this for
heathen Kings, what should we doe for Christian Princes?
If they have done this for glorye, what shoulde we doe for
religion? If they have done this without hope of heaven,
what should we doe that looke for immortalitie? And so
adding the encouragement of these exsamples, to the forward-
nes of their owne dispositions: what service is there in warre,
what honor in peace, which they will not be ready to doe, for
their worthy Queene? [1]

But the full sweep of North's devotion to Plutarch is
seen in his brief preface, "To the Reader." It is one of
the most impassioned defenses of history ever written,
and reveals in a few sentences the immense eagerness
with which England was absorbing the new learning. It
is no wonder that a gentleman and soldier like North
gave all his skill to translating such a work. For he believed

that there is no prophane studye better than Plutarke. All
other learning is private, fitter for Universities then cities,
fuller of contemplacion than experience, more commendable
in the students them selves, than profitable unto others.
Whereas stories are fit for every place, reache to all persons,
serve for all times, teache the living, revive the dead, so farre
excelling all other bookes, as it is better to see learning in
noble mens lives, than to reade it in Philosophers writings. [2]

It is not surprising that a man who could envisage the
destiny of history with so much imagination should be

[1] I, 4–5.   [2] I, 7.

able to make the heroes of antiquity come to life again in the likeness of English knights. And North's belief in the importance of reading Plutarch coincides with what had been the actual practice of his day, for Plutarch was studied with enthusiasm by both Philip Sidney and Henry of Navarre. The following are the forms in which the *Lives* played their chief part in molding the leaders of each nation:

Car on tiroit ce pauvre homme tout souillé de sang tirant aux traicts de la mort, & qui tendoit les deux mains à Cleopatra, & se soublevoit le mieulx qu'il pouvoit. C'estoit une chose bien malaisée que de le monter, mesmement à des femmes, toutefois Cleopatra en grande peine, s'efforceant de toute sa puissance, la teste courbée contre bas sans jamais lascher les cordes, feit tant à la fin qu'elle le monta & tira à soy, à l'aide de ceulx d'abas qui luy donnoyent courage, & tiroyent autant de peine à la voir ainsi travailler, comme elle mesme.[1] — VIII, 451.

For they plucked up poore Antonius all bloody as he was, and drawing on with pangs of death, who holding up his hands to Cleopatra, raised up him selfe as well as he could. It was a hard thing for these women to do, to lift him up: but Cleopatra stowping downe with her head, putting to all her strength to her uttermost power, did lift him up with much

---

[1] Amyot's closeness to the Greek can be illustrated here: πεφυρμένος γὰρ αἵματι καὶ δυσθανατῶν εἵλκετο, τὰς χεῖρας ὀρέγων εἰς ἐκείνην καὶ παραιωρούμενος. οὐ γὰρ ἦν γυναιξὶ ῥᾴδιον τὸ ἔργον, ἀλλὰ μόλις ἡ Κλεοπάτρα ταῖν χεροῖν ἐμπεφυκυῖα καὶ κατατεινομένη τῷ προσώπῳ τὸν δεσμὸν ἀνελάμβανεν, ἐπικελευομένων τῶν κάτοθεν αὐτῇ καὶ συναγωνιώντων. — *Plutarch's Lives*, Loeb Classical Library, ed. B. Perrin (New York, 1914), IX, 312. Perrin's literal translation is: "Smeared with blood and struggling with death he was drawn up, stretching out his hands to her even as he dangled in the air. For the task was not an easy one for women, and scarcely could Cleopatra, with clinging hands and strained face, pull up the rope, while those below called out encouragement to her and shared her agony." IX, 313.

a doe, and never let goe her hold, with the helpe of the women beneath that bad her be of good corage, and were as sorie to see her labor so, as she her selfe. — VI, 80.

North follows his model, cadence for cadence, and almost word for word; yet, with all this closeness, his work is as wholly English as Amyot's is wholly French. Each reflects the qualities of its translator. To point out North's differences from his model is the main ground of this essay. In the first place, the question arises whether North had a Greek or Latin text at his side, or whether he depended wholly upon Amyot. The English form of many of the names of tribes and places would not only suggest the latter alternative, but would indicate that North's acquaintance with both the classical languages was of the slightest. His general practice is either to use the French word, or to reconstruct a classical form, as it would seem, purely by guess. To take a few instances from the "Caesar": Amyot wrote "Milet," North makes it "Miletum" [1] instead of "Miletus." Similarly North writes "Oceanum" [2] for "Oceanus" (Fr. "Oceane"), "Hedui" [3] for "Aedui" (Fr. "Heduiens"), "Gomphes" [4] for "Gomphi" (Fr. "Gomphes"). He sometimes anglicizes Amyot's word directly with no effort at keeping a Latin ending: "Nervians" [5] for "Nervii" (Fr. "Nerviens"), and "Luke" [6] for "Luca"

[1] V, 2. [2] V, 12. [3] V, 28.
[4] V, 44. [5] V, 22.
[6] V, 23. Both these last two forms appear correctly as "Nervii" and "Luca" in the marginal notes. Such a discrepancy would suggest that these

(Fr. "Lucques"). In the "Coriolanus" Amyot unaccountably lost the first syllable of a word, and wrote "Vicaniens" as his translation of Λαουικάνους, (Latin "Lavicos"). North follows him with "Vicanians." [1] Similarly, where Amyot made a mistake in a proper name and wrote "Marcellus" instead of "Lentulus," and "Metellus" for "Tullius Cimber," North copies his error in both instances. [2]

On the other hand, there are plenty of scattered examples to indicate that the English translator referred on occasion to the Greek. For instance, in mentioning a quinsy that once kept Demosthenes from making a speech, he attempts an awkward pun that had been rejected by Amyot. [3] In the "Cicero" he gives in Greek

notes were not written by North, but inserted by the publisher for the reader's convenience. This belief is furthered by a great many other examples of the same sort, and by frequent mistakes. For instance, the note at V, 68, states "the murtherers of Caesar doe goe to the Capitoll" where the text says that they "went into the market place"; and the note at II, 153, "The tenth parte of the enemies goods offered Martius" is not equivalent to the "tenne of every sorte," which the text states was bestowed upon him.

[1] II, 176.

[2] V, 33, 67. On the basis of such mistranslated names, C. F. Tucker Brooke writes: "North seems never to have had recourse in case of difficulty to a Latin or Greek text of Plutarch." — *Shakespeare's Plutarch* (London, 1909), I, 193.

[3] "But wise men laughing at his fine excuse, tolde him it was no sinanche that had stopped his wesill that night, as he would make them beleve: but it was Harpalus argent-synanche," V, 305–306. Amyot expressed it thus: "Ce n'estoit pas une esquinance qui luy avoit estouppé la nuict le conduit de la voix, comme il vouloit faire à croire, mais que c'estoit l'argent qu'il avoit receu de Harpalus," VIII, 53. The Greek reads: οἱ δ' εὐφυεῖς Χλευάζοντες οὐχ ὑπὸ συνάγχης ἔφραζον, ἀλλ' ὑπ' ἀργυράγχης εἰλῆφθαι νύκτωρ τὸν δημαγωγόν, VII, 62.

characters, which Amyot had not used, the original forms
of certain Latin terms of philosophy.[1] In the "Pompey"
he quotes the Greek for "Let the dye be cast,"[2] which
had not appeared in the French. Furthermore, North
frequently introduces such Greek words as those for the
names of the months: "The kings of Macedon did never
use to put their armie into the field in the moneth of
Dason, which is June."[3] Again, in a few places where
North mistakes the sense, the confusion may be due to
his having tried to supplement the French with the
Greek. Take this sentence, which begins ambiguously
and ends in absurdity: "Many writers doe agree, that
Porus was foure cubits and a shaft length hier and bigger
then the Elephant, although the Elephant was very
great, and as bigge as a horse."[4] The French is perfectly straightforward:[5] Porus was four cubits and a
half in height, and, although seated on a large elephant,
his size was proportionate to his mount. There is no
mention of a horse. But the Greek contains a phrase
stating that the elephant made as fit a steed for Porus as
a horse for a horseman.[6] North's disaster may have resulted from his effort at combining the two.

[1] V, 356.   [2] Ἀνεῤῥίφθω κύβος, IV, 271.
[3] IV, 314. Also, "Let them call it the second moneth, Artemisium, which
is Maye," *Ibid.* The Greek forms here are Δαισίον and Ἀρτεμίσιον. They
do not appear in Amyot.
[4] IV, 369.   [5] VII, 148.
[6] Οἱ δὲ πλεῖστοι τῶν συγγραφέων ὁμολογοῦσι τὸν Πῶρον ὑπεραίροντα τεσσά-
ρων πηχῶν σπιθαμῇ τὸ μῆκος ἱππότου μηδὲν ἀποδεῖν πρὸς τὸν ἐλέφαντα συμμετρίᾳ
διὰ τὸ μέγεθος καὶ τὸν ὄγκον τοῦ σώματος. καίτοι μέγιστος ἦν ὁ ἐλέφας, VII, 396.

But, on the whole, it is evident that, although North had scattered recourse to the original, he depended on it very little. He relied on Amyot, and, in the few cases where the Frenchman had failed, he went down also. And being by no means a complete scholar, he naturally made errors of his own. His work is far less finished than Amyot's. He is less precise and often loses the rhythm of a phrase, as in the description of Brutus as "well-beloved of the people and his owne" [1] instead of "bien voulu du peuple, aimé des siens." [2] But when his constructions are clumsy or loose, the usual reason is that he has followed the French too closely. Hence the vagueness of Brutus' declaration to Cicero, "And, for his owne part, that he had never resolutely determined with him selfe to make warre, or peace, but otherwise, that he was certenly minded never to be slave nor subject." [3] This rendering lacks both the clearness and the energy of the original, the words of which it blindly follows.

In addition to being over-literal, North is sometimes misled by ambiguity in the French. Not inexcusably is "celle de Pompeius" [4] rendered by "Pompey's wife," [5] though it should be "Pompey's daughter." It is less excusable, however, when North translates "le chemin qui s'appelle la voye d'Appius" [6] as "the highway going

---

[1] VI, 210.   [2] IX, 161.

[3] VI, 203 ("Et que de sa part il n'avoit jamais resoluement arresté en soymesme de faire ny la paix, ny la guerre, mais que sa resolution et sa deliberation arrestée estoit de jamais ne servir," IX, 149).

[4] VII, 210.   [5] V, 14.   [6] VII, 194.

unto Appius," [1] instead of "the Appian way." But he is
rarely betrayed into any serious mistake. In an account
of Pompey's dream he leaves out several sentences of
Amyot as well as the Frenchman's note that the passage
was defective in the Greek.[2] He takes the object for the
subject when he writes, "Caesar dyed at six and fifty
yeres of age: and Pompey also lived not passing foure
yeares more than he." [3] He is also confused by the order
of words when he says, "There were few Senators that
would be President of the Senate under him," [4] where
the French reads: "Il y eut peu des senateurs qui se vou-
lussent trouver soubz luy President au senat." [5]

It is extraordinary how North's inaccuracies sometimes improve the context rather than injure it. "He
was somewhat geven to be redde faced, and had a payer
of staring eyes in his heade," [6] is not quite accurate for
"Il estoit un peu roux de visage, & avoit les yeux pers," [7]
but it gives us a vivid picture of Cato. The remark that
the excitement of a charge acts on soldiers "as a boxe of
the eare that settes men a fire," [8] is very suggestive, although the real sense of the French word "soufflet" [9]
here happens to be "bellows." "His familier friendes
above all rebuked him, saying he was to be accompted

---

[1] V, 5. These last two mistakes are both corrected in the edition of 1603.
[2] V, 44.
[3] V, 70 ("Et ne survescut Pompeius gueres plus de quatre ans," VII, 319).
[4] V, 15.   [5] VII, 212.   [6] III, 2.
[7] III, 437.   [8] V, 46.
[9] "Comme un soufflet qui l'allume," VII, 273. The simile is not in the
Greek.

no better than a beast," [1] is certainly a strong equivalent for "qu'il seroit bien beste." [2] And the passage in the "Publicola" telling how the conspirators swore a "great and horrible othe, drincking the bloude of a man *and shaking hands in his bowells*," [3] adds an intensity of horror beyond that of "touchant des mains aux entrailles." [4] It is hard to believe that such a stroke represents an unconscious error and not deliberate artistry.

Even the enumeration of North's mistakes shows his closeness to the French, for in the extent of a large folio their slight bulk is hardly to be noticed. But the thing that strikes the attention at every turn is the many passages which have a wholly English sound.

We be sometime so ravished with delight and pleasure at the hearing of the talke of some wise, discreete, and well spoken old man, from whose mouth there floweth a streame of speech sweeter than honnie, in rehearsing the adventures which he hath had in his greene and youthfull yeares, the paines that he hath indured, and the perills that he hath overpassed, so as we perceive not how the time goeth away [5]

possesses a simplicity almost Biblical, and yet is an exact reproduction from Amyot's "Aux Lecteurs." [6] Similar magic acts upon these words of Coriolanus:

[1] I, 222.   [2] I, 348.   [3] I, 252.
[4] I, 403.   [5] I, 16–17.
[6] "Nous sommes quelquefois si ravis d'aise & de joye, que nous ne sentons point le cours des heures, en oyant deviser un sage, disert & eloquent viellard, en la bouche duquel sourt un flux de langue plus doulx que miel, quand il va recitant les adventures qu'il a euës en ses verds & jeunes ans, les travaux qu'il a endurez, & les perilz qu'il a passez," I, xxxiii.

Ce que Martius ne pouvant supporter, la releva tout aussi tost en s'escriant: 'O mere, que m'as tu fait?' & en luy serrant estroitement la main droite: 'Ha, dit il, mere, tu as vaincu un victoire heureuse pour ton pais, mais bien malheureuse & mortelle pour ton filz.' — II, 512–513.

Martius seeing that, could refraine no longer, but went straight and lifte her up, crying out: Oh mother, what have you done to me? And holding her hard by the right hande, oh mother, sayed he, you have wonne a happy victorie for your countrie, but mortall and unhappy for your sonne. — II, 186.

Varying from the French in no detail, North made the passage so completely English that it was able to fire Shakespeare's imagination for one of the greatest speeches of his play:

> Coriolanus (*holding Volumnia by the hand, silent*).
>   O mother, mother!
> What have you done?   Behold, the heavens do ope,
> The gods look down, and this unnatural scene
> They laugh at.   O my mother! mother! O!
> You have won a happy victory to Rome;
> But, for your son, believe it, O, believe it,
> Most dangerously you have with him prevail'd,
> If not most mortal to him.   (V, iii.)

V

That there is a subtle difference between Amyot and North, that their pulses do not beat at the same rate, is at once apparent if we read several pages first of the one and then of the other.   Montaigne spoke of "the pure elegancy" of Amyot's speech, and of "the unsearchable depth of his knowledge."   The tribute is just, but these

are not the words which we should use to describe North.
Yet only by the keenest attention can we discover the
full cause of the difference between the two. To begin
with, a careful examination reveals that, notwithstanding the literalness of his translation, North displays all
the habits of Elizabethan speech. Nouns do the work of
verbs at will: "to pleasure his friends," [1] "They say his
enemies did malice him." [2] Amyot had not been shy of
using doublets for the sake of his rhythm, but North
increases their numbers: [3] "stowtly and resolutely" [4]
for "courageusement," [5] "protectour and defendour" [6]
for "tutrice," [7] "Cato in contrary maner brought downe
all that excesse and superfluitie unto a *marvelous neere and*
uncredible savinge," [8] for "luy au contraire y feit un
changement de superfluité excessive en simplicité in-
croyable." [9]

But North's love of fullness is restrained, and he very
seldom introduces so much as an original clause relevant
to the situation, as when he writes how the Persian courtiers "greatly envied him, *and afterwardes murmured
much against him*" [10] for "luy porterent depuis grande
envie." [11] Alliteration happily found its way into his

---

[1] III, 16.   [2] III, 12.

[3] On the other hand, North sometimes reverses the process and reduces
Amyot's doublets, thus: "goodly persuasions," I, 296, for "les belles raisons
& remonstrances," II, 30; "the greatest comfort," IV, 334, for "du plus
grand reconfort, & de la plus doulce consolation," VII, 80; "so pacient," I,
295, for "une si grande facilité, & si grande patience," II, 28.

[4] I, 294.   [5] II, 26.   [6] I, 293.   [7] II, 24.
[8] III, 10.   [9] III, 453.   [10] I, 315.   [11] II, 64.

pages: "watche and warde upon the walles"; [1] "Under the gentle name of a colonie they would cloke and culler the most cruell and unnaturall facte"; [2] the corn "should be devided by the polle, without paying any pennie." [3] North sometimes varies the words: when Amyot repeats "Tu sois un jour quelque grand bien, ou quelque grand mal," [4] it seems more natural for him to write "One daye thou shalt doe some *notable good* thing, or some *extreme* mischief." [5] And to how great an extent the English translator shares the gift of his time for striking compounds is clear from his rendering of Caesar's remark: "Je . . . me deffie . . . de ces maigres & pasles là" [6] by "These pale visaged and carrion leane people, I feare them most." [7]

North also employs verbal phrases which suggest the picture of an action: "being come nowe to the swordes pointe," [8] for "donques arrivé sur le bord du peril"; [9] or "We must all laye our heades together," [10] for "Il fault donc que nous advisons tous ensemble." [11] When Themistocles' schoolmasters had him study any book that dealt with matters of state, North records how "he would beate at it marvelously," [5] whereas the French had stated merely "qu'il le notoit." [4] Corio-

---

[1] II, 180 ("à defendre les murailles," II, 503).

[2] II, 157 ("couvroyent la plus inhumaine cruaulté du monde soubs le doulx & gracieux nom de colonie," II, 462).

[3] II, 161 ("par teste en rien faire payer," II, 469).

[4] II, 5.   [5] I, 283.   [6] VII, 307.

[7] V, 64.   [8] I, 312.   [9] II, 59.

[10] I, 300.   [11] II, 38.

lanus, in the words of Amyot, spoke with "un ton de voix forte," with the result that "le peuple s'aigrit & irrita fort asprement contre luy." [1] But North says that he "gave him selfe in his wordes to thunder," which "stirred coales emong the people, who were in wonderfull furie at it." [2]

The Elizabethan loved a precise detail that brought a glowing reality to his words. Where the Greek had begun a speech with Ἄνθρωπε,[3] and Amyot had written "Vieillard,"[4] North, centering on the specific, says, "O gray bearde." [5] Such changes are very frequent. Amyot declared: "Car il n'est pas raisonnable d'user des choses qui ont vie & sentiment, tout ainsi que nous ferions d'un soulier, ou de quelque autre utensile, en les jettant après qu'elles sont toutes usées & rompues de nous avoir servis." [6] North concentrates on the simile and gives it fullness: "And there is no reason, to use livinge and sencible thinges, as we woulde use an *olde* shooe *or a ragge*: to cast it out *apon the dongehill* when we have worne it, and can serve us no longer." [7] These details may seem very slight, but they leave an indelible mark upon North's prose. He has a great gift for figurative language. He tells how the Consul went up to the chair of state, and then "spake to Martius whose valliantnes he commended *beyond the moone*." [8] The French says that he "exalta la vertu à merveilles." [9] When Coriolanus

[1] II, 474.	[2] II, 164.	[3] II, 328.
[4] III, 462.	[5] III, 14.	[6] III, 452.
[7] III, 9.	[8] II, 153.	[9] II, 455.

brought back his army "safe and sounde to Rome, and every man riche and loden with spoyle: then the home-tarriers and housedoves that kept Rome still, beganne to repent them that it was not their happe to goe with him." [1] For "hometarriers and housedoves" the French contains merely "les autres." [2]

Wholly English, too, is North's colloquial tone. The statement that "Alexander frowning upon Philotas brought all his enemies upon his backe" [3] is quite another matter from "Il incita ceulx qui de longue main luy vouloyent mal." [4] He "dyd cast him in the teethe" [5] has a dramatic turn that is absent from "luy reprocha." [6] "She dyd nothing but fill her bellie" [7] is on a totally different plane of expression from "Elle ne faisoit rien que . . . faire bonne chere." [6] The difference may be emphasized by two examples from the schoolboy quarrel between Cassius and Faustus. "Cassius rose up on his feete and gave him two good whirts on the eare" [8] is North's translation of "Cassius se dressant en pieds luy donna une couple de souflets." [9] "Goe to Faustus, speake againe and thou darest . . . that my fistes may walke once againe about thine eares" [10] is his rendering for "Or sus, Faustus, prens encore la hardiesse de redire

---

[1] II, 158. This is a favorite figure with North. In the "Themistocles," speaking about the treatment of the Persian women he writes, "No man ever seeth them abroad at any time, but are allwayes *like housedoves* kept within doores," I, 312.

[2] II, 463.   [3] IV, 356.   [4] VII, 123.
[5] I, 302–303.   [6] II, 42.   [7] I, 303.
[8] VI, 189.   [9] IX, 123.   [10] VI, 189.

une autre fois . . . à celle fin que de rechef je te rompe
la teste à coups de poing." [1] North's construction is
close to his original, but the guiding principle of Amyot's
sentence was dignity and restraint, neither of which
finds much reflection in the Englishman's picturesque
vigor.

For North's words are often the words of the street.
The speech of his characters is actual speech. Such realistic phrases as "Tushe, sayd he," "Go thy way," "I
warrant you," "Mary, said Cato," appear without any
suggestion from either Plutarch or Amyot. Direct discourse frequently takes the place of indirect: "The King
saluted him, and spake very curteously to him, saying:
I am nowe your dettor of two hundred talents" [2] for
"Le roy le salua, & luy parla amiablement, disant que
ja il luy devoit deux cents talents." [3] The nuances of a
speaker's voice and tone are reproduced. In his conversation with the Persian monarch, Themistocles ad-
dresses his Majesty with more terms of reverence and
praise in the English version: "Maye it please your
majestie, O noble king" [4] are his opening words instead
of "Sire roy." [5] He continues in the same elaborate
manner: "You will *of your princely grace* use my *harde*
fortune as a *good* occasion to shewe your *honourable*
vertue." [6] And when the nobles run to the aid of Corio-

[1] IX, 123–124.   [2] I, 315.   [3] II, 63.
[4] I, 313.   [5] II, 60.
[6] I, 314 ("Tu vueilles user de ma fortune comme d'une occasion & matiere
de monstrer ta vertu," II, 61).

lanus "avec grands cris," [1] in North the actual sound of
their voices is heard: they "beganne to crie alowde,
Helpe Martius." [2]

North also draws into his prose a rich store of proverbial phrases. "But this holdeth no water" [3] is the way
he expresses "Mais ilz ne disent pas la verité." [4] Pompey
"did lay all the irons in the fire he could, to bring it to
passe that he might be chosen Dictator" [5] adds color to
"procurast toutes les choses qui pouvoyent servir à
ceste fin." [6] But the greatest glory of the translator's
vocabulary is his magnificent slang. A favorite expression is "in hugger mugger": Antony's decision that
Caesar's body "should be honorably buried, and not in
hugger mugger." [7] Another favorite is the word "marvelous": the battle was "marvelous bloudie"; [8] "a marvelous great thunder"; [9] Themistocles was "marvelous
angry in his minde." [10] Other expressions are even
racier: the Spartans "dyd sit on his skirtes" [11] is the way
he expresses the idea that "those of Sparta pursued
him." The honey-tongued orators of the Senate, "tous
ces autres gracieux," [12] are called "these meale mouthed
men." [13] "Emporta la victoire" [14] becomes on one occa-

---

[1] II, 475.   [2] II, 164.   [3] VI, 189.
[4] IX, 123.   [5] V, 30-31.   [6] VII, 243.
[7] VI, 200 ("et non point à cachettes," IX, 144).
[8] II, 153.
[9] IV, 331 ("un si violent orage de tonnerre," VII, 74).
[10] I, 296 ("fort marry," II, 30).
[11] I, 308 (Amyot, II, 51).
[12] III, 482.   [13] III, 24.   [14] VII, 162.

sion "bare the bel." [1] And when it is recounted how Cato's words had the power to touch men's hearts so that tears came to their eyes and their wills could be turned in whatever direction he chose, North writes: "He could make men water their plantes that hearde him, and leade them as he would by the eare." [2]

All these qualities of the translator's language and vocabulary go into his verse as well as into his prose. The result is often energetic:

> But in the ende (O right reward for such)
> this bribing wretch was forced for to holde
> a tipling bowthe, most like a clowne or snutche. [3]

Not until you stop to consider that these are Timocreon's lines on Themistocles do you realize the incongruity. Homer is treated just as freely:

> Tush, meddle thou with weighing duly out
> Thy maids their task, and pricking on a clout. [4]

And when North describes an incident of the Gymnopoedia — "the which Sophocles doth easely declare by these verses":

> The songe which you shall singe, shalbe the sonnet sayde,
> by Hermionè lusty lasse, that strong and sturdy mayde:

[1] IV, 376.
[2] III, 10 ("Qui attaignoyent si bien les cueurs au vif, qu'elles faisoyent venir les larmes aux yeux des escoutans, & tournoyent les hommes en tel sens comme il vouloit," III, 455).
[3] I, 306 (Amyot, II, 48).
[4] VI, 204.

Which trust her petticote, about her middle shorte,
    and set to shewe her naked hippes, in francke and frendly
    sorte,[1] —

the notion that the verses have any relation to the Greek is utterly grotesque. Even though North did furnish Shakespeare with the four lines for Timon's epitaph,[2] he had no talent for verse. The best that can be said for him is that Amyot is hardly closer to the spirit of the Greek, and lacks the Englishman's robust animation. But if the full Elizabethan qualities of North's style only make his efforts at poetry extravagant and ridiculous, no such criticism can touch his prose.

There is a directness in his work that cuts through all inessentials. Perhaps this is indicated by the difference in sound and temper between "Ces paroles emeurent grandement à compassion le cueur d'Alexandre"[3] and "These words pearced Alexanders hart."[4] There is no

---

[1] I, 203. Amyot's version is:
    "Vous chanterez la robuste pucelle
    Hermioné, la cotte de laquelle
    Sans rien cacher à l'entour de la cuisse,
    Qui sort dehors toute nue, se plisse." (I, 312.)

[2] The lines appear as two epitaphs in North, VI, 74:
    "Heere lyes a wretched corse, of wretched soule bereft,
        Seeke not my name: a plague consume you wicked wretches
        left."

    "Heere lye I Timon who alive all living men did hate,
        Passe by, and curse thy fill: but passe, and stay not here thy
        gate."
Shakespeare changed "wicked wretches" in the second line to "wicked caitiffs," and ran the four lines together (*Timon of Athens*, V, v). In Amyot each epitaph had been a quatrain.

[3] VII, 165.   [4] IV, 377.

mincing of words: "He aunswered the messenger that brought him these newes, he should tell Parmenio that he was a mad man and out of his wits"[1] ("que Parmenion n'estoit pas en son bon sens, ains estoit troublé de son entendement"[2]); or Statilius' declaration to Brutus "that it were an unwise parte of him, to put his life in daunger, for a sight of ignorant fooles and asses"[3] ("pour des folz & des ignorans"[4]). North also has a poignancy never quite touched by Amyot, although he changed the words very slightly to achieve it. Set side by side the two versions of Alexander's death: something in North's blunt vigor makes the fact more real to the imagination:

Mais Aristobulus met, qu'ayant une fiebvre violente & une alteration extreme, il beut du vin, dont il commencea à entrer en resverie, & à la fin en mourut le trentieme jour du mois de juin. — VII, 177.	But Aristobulus writeth, that he had such an extreame fever and *thirst withall*, that he dranke wine, and after that fel *a raving*, and at the length dyed the thirtie day of the month of June. — IV, 384.

One reason why North could write so vitally was because he had fully assimilated Plutarch's matter. The translator's belief in the important part that history should play in man's life found its perfect illustration in his own. His words fused with his experience. He did not resurrect dead Plutarch; his imagination recreated the heroes of antiquity in the environment of England. His language — and theirs — is that of an English cap-

---

[1] IV, 337.   [2] VII, 86.   [3] VI, 192.   [4] IX, 128.

tain. Eurybiades was "a rancke coward at time of neede"[1] ("homme à qui le cueur failloit au besoing"[2]). Xerxes' admiral "was by them valliantly receyved upon their pikes, and thrust over borde into the sea"[3] ("Mais eulx le soustindrent hardiment, & à coups de javeline le renverserent en la mer"[4]). "The barbarous King understanding these newes, was so affrayed, that he hoysed away with all possible speede"[5] (". . . se partit à la plus grande diligence qui luy fut possible"[6]). When Philopoemon, wounded with a dart that "pierced both sides through and through," realized that the terrible fight would soon be over, Amyot said "qu'il perdoit patience de despit."[7] But North adds: "it spited him to the guttes, he would so faine have been among them."[8] The account of a battle takes the translator's mind into a realm of experience untouched by Amyot. North follows his text closely most of the way, but he cannot help bringing in phrases that the deeds of Hawkins and Frobisher were making common on men's lips:

La grande multitude des vaisseaux, ny la pompe & magnificence des paremens d'iceulx, ny les cris superbes & chants de victoire des Barbares, ne servent de rien a l'encontre de ceulx qui ont le cueur de joindre de près, & combatre à coups de main leur ennemy, & qu'il ne fault point faire de compte de tout cela, ains

It was not the great multitude of shippes, nor the pompe and *sumptuous* setting out of the same, nor the prowde barbarous showts and songes of victorie that could stande them to purpose against *noble* harts *and valliant minded souldiers*, that durst grapple with them, and come to hands strokes with their en-

[1] I, 295. [2] II, 27. [3] I, 299. [4] II, 35.
[5] I, 301. [6] II, 39. [7] IV, 16. [8] III, 54.

aller droit affronter les hommes & s'attacher hardiment à eulx. — II, 19-20.

emies: and that they should make no reckoning of all that *bravery and bragges*, but should sticke to it like men, and *laye it on the jacks of them.*—I, 290-291.

Not only in the description of battles did the man of action have the advantage of the bishop. North took the whole book from the study to the camp. When it is remarked of Alexander, "Aussi estoit il fort sobre de sa bouche quant au manger," [1] the English reads, "He was also no greedy gutte," [2] and we can hear the rough talk of a soldiers' board. No one but a horseman could describe Bucephalus so fitly: "The horse was found so rough and churlish that the ryders said he would never do service, for he would let no man get up on his backe nor abide any of the gentlemens voyces about king Philip, but would yerke out at them." [3] And the air of Plymouth or Dover comes to our nostrils when we hear phrases like "staye following him at the poope" [4] ("qu'ilz ne le poursuyvissent incontinent," [5]) "fall upon the lee shore for harborow" [6] ("abordassent & se retirassent à l'abry" [7]), or "There were 200 sayle that went to cast about the Ile of Sciathe, and so to come in" [8] ("Qu'il y en avoit encore autres deux cents, qui alloyent faire le tour par dessus l'isle de Sciathe" [9]).

In other ways, partly deliberate, partly unconscious, North has transformed Plutarch into an Englishman.

[1] VII, 58.   [2] IV, 323.   [3] IV, 303 (Amyot, VII, 18).
[4] I, 301.   [5] II, 39.   [6] I, 292.
[7] II, 21.   [8] I, 290.   [9] II, 18.

Following the lead of Amyot, he modernizes the pagan religion, without worrying about anachronisms.   He even goes beyond the Frenchman in this respect.   "Le deluge" is always written "Noe's flood."   "The Nunne which pronounced the oracles" [1] is his equivalent of "la prophetisse." [2]   He causes Alexander to condemn "that vile Tarentin marchaunt Theodorus and his marchaundise to the Devill," [3] where His Satanic Majesty is not specified by Amyot's "à la malheure." [4]   Furthermore, English customs crop up on every page.   "Having a pece of lande he would sell, he willed the crier to proclaime open sale of it in the market place, and with all he should adde unto the sale, that his lande laye by a good neighbour" [5] sounds as authentic as if it had come from a sixteenth-century account book, instead of being a saying of Themistocles.   The tang of "all the feasts and common sports were in their greatest ruffe" [6] is wholly Elizabethan; and so, naturally, when one of these common sports is named, it is contemporary too, and Alexander plays at tennis. [7]   And whenever the matter deals with kings and queens and customs of the court, it is not antiquity, nor the ceremonious Court of France, but the free and hearty days of Elizabeth that come to the reader's mind.   For instance, take the implications of

[1] IV, 312.   [2] VII, 37.   [3] IV, 323.   [4] VII, 57.
[5] I, 303 ("En faisant proclamer un sien heritage qu'il vouloit vendre il, commanda au sergent qui faisoit la criée, d'adjouxter à sa proclamation, que l'heritage avoit bon voisin," II, 43).
[6] V, 6 ("en leur plus grande vogue," VII, 195).   [7] IV, 345.

this statement: "Then having ended these doleful plaints, and crowned the tombe with garlands and sundry nosegayes, and marvelous lovingly imbraced the same: she commaunded they should prepare her bath, and when she had bathed and washed her selfe, she fell to her meate, and was sumptuously served." [1] Such words may not express the dignity of a princess "descended of so many royal kings," but they burst with an energy that needed little sublimation to embody the spirit of Shakespeare's Egypt.

When all details have been listed, the outstanding reason for North's greatness is that his own personality found expression in his work. The present-day translator of the classics aims at a literal rendering of each word and phrase; he does not intrude his personality, but tries to reproduce his author faultlessly. The difference between his work and North's is like that between photography and painting. The one is a useful record; the other has an independent life of its own. North, separated though he is from the original by Amyot's French, is never very far from the matter of Plutarch. And this matter is given new fire by the fact that in subtle, almost impalpable ways, the translator fuses with it the robust temper of his age.

[1] VI, 86 ("Après avoir fait telles lamentations, et qu'elle eut couronné le tumbeau de bouquets, festons & chappeaux de fleurs, & qu'elle l'eut embrassé fort affecteusement, elle commanda qu'on luy apprestast un baing: puis quand elle se fut baignée & lavée, elle se meit à table, où elle fut servie magnifiquement," VIII, 462).

We have the completely Elizabethan point of view when North describes the soothsayers, "ces gens de religion," [1] as "all this goodly rable of superstition and priestes." [2] It sounds as though this devoted adherent of the Queen will allow no remarks to be made against a monarchy when the description of Antony is changed from "un homme insolent, & qui de sa nature favorisoit à la monarchie" [3] to "a wicked man, and that in nature favored tyranny." [4] National pride finds its expression when he adds an adjective to the description of Britain, and slurs over the mention of its conquest by Caesar: "For he was the first that sailed the west Ocean with an army by sea . . . to make warre in that so great *and famous* Ilande . . . and was the first that enlarged the Romane Empire, beyonde the earth inhabitable." [5] ("Car ce fut luy premier qui navigua l'Ocean occidental avec armée navale . . . pour aller faire la guerre en ceste isle si grande . . . & luy fut le premier qui commencea *à la conquerir*, & qui estendit l'empire Romain plus avant que le rond de la terre habitable." [6])

In addition, North's language reveals many of the personal characteristics of the English gentleman of the day. At times he is blunt: when Themistocles boasted that he could make a small city great, although he could not tune a viol or play a psalterion, Amyot rendered the opinion of the cultured Plutarch that his words were

---

[1] II, 503.   [2] II, 180.   [3] IX, 140.
[4] VI, 198.   [5] V, 25.   [6] VII, 231–232.

"un peu haultaines & odieuses." [1] But North, the man of action, approves them; for him they are "great and stout words." [2] He is a choleric moralist who will stand no nonsense: Phoea "was surnamed a sowe for her beastly brutishe behaviour, and wicked life." [3] At other times he shows something of the Englishman's chivalry: he often has a peculiar gentleness when he writes about women. His emphasis is on the "goodliness" and "sweetness" of their beauty: "their sweete faire faces" [4] for "leurs belles faces." [5] In the poignant description of the living burial of unchaste vestal virgins, North renders literally almost every word except "la criminelle" [6] which he changes to "the seely offendour." [7] But you would know he was talking of a whore when he tells how Thais "finely praising Alexander, and partely in sporting wise, began to utter matter in affection of her countrie, but yet of greater importance *than became her mouth*." [8] This moral severity causes him to expurgate shamelessly: Flora's parting caress to Pompey is called "a sweete quippe or pleasaunt taunte." [9] Fortunately

---

[1] II, 6.

[2] I, 283.

[3] I, 37 ("Elle fut surnommée Laie, pour ses meurs deshonnestes & sa meschante vie," I, 17).

[4] IV, 322.   [5] VII, 57.

[6] I, 272.   [7] I, 181.

[8] IV, 343 (". . . mais bien de plus grande consequence qu'il ne luy appartenoit," VII, 99).

[9] IV, 207 (In the French she said "qu'il estoit impossible quand elle couchoit avec luy, qu'elle s'en departit sans le mordre," VI, 105).

such instances are not frequent enough to form a blemish on his book.[1]

North's translation is constantly colored by his feeling. The slight additions that he makes to the story of Alexander's dog indicate that he dwelt upon the details lovingly: "It is reported also, that having lost a dogge of his called Peritas, which he had brought uppe *of a whelpe*, and loved *very dearely*: he built also a citie, and called it after his name." [2] Here is an intimacy of tone and a stir of emotion that do not appear in the reserved classic pages of Amyot, or, for that matter, of Plutarch either. The whole difference in temper between the French and English can be suggested by a single phrase. When the mother of Coriolanus received her son after a victory, Amyot stated that she had "les larmes aux yeux espraintes de joye." [3] But in the words of North she stands "with teares *ronning downe* her cheekes for joye." [4]

North's imagination crystallizes a phrase into a picture. Where Amyot spoke of "d'escrimeurs à oultrance," [5] he writes "the cruell fight of fencers at unrebated swordes." [6] He instinctively seizes the dramatic

---

[1] The statement, "Lucius Quintius caried ever with him a younge boye to the warres," III, 24, omits "dont il avoit abusé charnellement des enfance du garcon." There are a number of cases where North omits a detail of this sort, but his words nearly always leave apparent the whole implication of the situation.

[2] IV, 370 ("un chien nommé Peritas, qu'il avoit nourry & qu'il amoit," VII, 150).

[3] II, 444. [4] II, 147. [5] II, 459. [6] II, 155.

elements of a situation and heightens them. For example, note the rhetorical stir in Volumnia's words: "For the bitter soppe of most harde choyce is offered thy wife and children, to forgoe the one of the two: either to lose the persone of thy selfe, or the nurse of their native contrie." [1] It is absent from "pour ce qu'il est forcé à ta femme & à tes enfans qu'ilz soyent privez de l'un des deux, ou de toy, ou de leur pais." [2] Sometimes this dramatic heightening leads to extravagance, as when Cleopatra, appearing before Caesar after Antony's death, is described as having "the most parte of her stomake torne in sunder." [3] But usually it is both bold and stirring, a rare gift of imagination that enhances the power of North's prose.

It also made his book ready to the dramatist's hand. Caesar "when he sawe Brutus with his sworde drawen . . . pulled his gowne over his heade, and made no more resistaunce, and was driven either casually, or purposedly, by the counsell of the conspirators, against the base whereupon Pompeys image stoode, which *ranne* all of *a goare* bloude, *till he was slaine*." [4] Amyot's concluding words read simply: ". . . contre la base, sur laquelle estoit posée l'image de Pompeius, qui en fut toute en-

---

[1] II, 184.   [2] II, 510.

[3] VI, 84 ("la plus grande partie de son estomac deschiré & meurtry," VIII, 459, is also a heightening of the Greek, of which the modern literal reading is "There were also visible many marks of the cruel blows upon her bosom").

[4] V, 68.

sanglantée." [1] North's stroke of genius, for it is no less, could not be improved by Shakespeare when he wrote how

> in his mantle muffling up his face,
> Even at the base of Pompey's statuë,
> Which all the while ran blood, great Caesar fell. [2]

VI

The translator's words had fitted Plutarch's matter exactly to Shakespeare's purpose. This is not the place to go over the well-known ground of the dramatist's debt to Plutarch, [3] but a few indications of the extent to which he used North's book will immediately crystallize our conception of the translator's importance for sixteenth-century England. North did not stand in the same category as Holinshed, since he not only afforded Shakespeare the material for his plots, but also gave him living characters in their full stature. More significant still, his very words satisfied the dramatist's need. Many books can provide a poet with his material; only the rarest can so inflame his imagination that he will take over entire passages, simply changing the cadence from prose to verse. How deeply North's words had sunk into Shakespeare's mind is perhaps clearest from those passages where he retained the translator's diction, even when applying it to a new purpose of his own.

[1] VII, 315.
[2] *Julius Caesar*, III, ii.
[3] See C. F. Tucker Brooke, *Shakespeare's Plutarch*.

For instance, where North had written that "a goodly horse with a capparison" [1] was offered to Coriolanus, at the same juncture Shakespeare makes Lartius say:

> O General,
> Here is the steed, we the caparison. [2]

The full reason why North blends so easily into drama lies in the peculiar way in which he has raised the emotional pitch of the original. Take the famous visit of Coriolanus to Tullus Aufidius:

> It was even twy light when he entred the cittie of Antium, and many people met him in the streetes, but no man knewe him. So he went directly to Tullus Aufidius house, and when he came thither, he got him up straight to the chimney harthe, and sat him downe, and spake not a worde to any man, his face all muffled over. They of the house spying him, wondered what he should be, and yet they durst not byd him rise. For ill favoredly muffled and disguised as he was, yet there appeared a certaine majestie in his countenance, and in his silence: whereupon they went to Tullus who was at supper, to tell him of the straunge disguising of this man. [3]

The French for this passage is more concise and tightly drawn, [4] but it has not the same atmosphere of suspense. "Ceulx de la maison," which accurately reproduces οἱ δὲ κατὰ τὴν οἰκίαν, [5] is the ground on which North builds his suggestive phrase "They of the house spying him," the idea of spying being his own. A similar hint of dramatic intensity lies in "ill favoredly muffled up and dis-

---

[1] II, 153. [2] *Coriolanus*, I, ix.
[3] II, 169. [4] II, 484.   [5] IV, 172.

guised as he was." Amyot has a plain "encore qu'il se
cachast," and the idea was expressed by nothing more
than a particle in the Greek ἦν γάρ τι καὶ περὶ αὐτὸν. And
the concluding words, "the straunge disguising of this
man," again center the attention on the mysterious
figure of Coriolanus by the hearth. The original τὴν
ἀτοπίαν τοῦ πράγματος, which Amyot mirrors in "ceste
estrange façon de faire," is a general statement de-
void of the bright glowing suggestion of North's detail. North's imagination has set the stage, and his
words beat at such a dramatic pitch that when Aufidius
enters and Coriolanus reveals himself, Shakespeare has
simply to paraphrase him:

> Coriolanus (*unmuffling*). *If, Tullus,*
> *Not yet thou know'st me, and seeing me, dost not*
> Think *me for the man I am,* necessity
> Commands me name *myself. . . .*
> My name is *Caius Marcius, who hath done*
> *To* thee *particularly, and to all the Volsces,*
> *Great hurt and mischief;* thereto witness may
> *My surname, Coriolanus: the painful service,*
> *The extreme dangers,* and the drops of blood
> Shed for my thankless country, are requited
> *But* with that *surname; a good memory,*
> *And witness of the malice and displeasure*
> Which *thou shouldst bear me: only* that *name remains;*
> *The cruelty and envy of the people,*
> Permitted *by* our *dastard nobles, who*
> Have all *forsook me,* hath devour'd *the rest;*
> *And* suffer'd *me by the* voice of slaves *to be*
> Whoop'd out of Rome. *Now this extremity*
> *Hath* brought *me to thy hearth; not* out *of hope,*

Mistake me not, *to save my life; for if*
I had fear'd death, of all the men i' the world
I would have 'voided thee; *but* in mere *spite*
To be full quit of those my *banishers,*
Stand I before thee here.[1]   (IV, v.)

VII

North's *Plutarch* enjoyed a sustained popularity.   A
second edition appeared in 1595, a third in 1603 with the
addition of fifteen new lives, not written by Plutarch,
but "englished," according to the title-page, by the
same translator.[2]   Reprints of this last edition were

[1] I have italicized all the words used by North. His passage reads: "Then
Martius unmuffled him selfe, and after he had paused a while, making no
answer, he sayed unto him: If thou knowest me not yet, Tullus, and seeing
me, dost not perhappes beleeve me to be the man I am in dede, I must of
necessitie bewraye my selfe to be that I am. I am Caius Martius, who hath
done to thy selfe particularly, and to all the Volsces generally, great hurte
and mischief, which I cannot denie for my surname of Coriolanus that I
beare. For I never had other benefit nor recompence, of all the true and
paynefull service I have done, and the extreme daungers I have bene in, but
this only surname: a good memorie and witnes, of the malice and displeasure
thou showldest beare me. In deede the name only remaineth with me: for the
rest, the envie and crueltie of the people of Rome have taken from me, by the
sufferance of the dastardly nobilitie and magistrates, who have forsaken me,
and let me be banished by the people. This extremitie hath now driven me to
come as a poore suter, to take thy chimney harthe, not out of any hope I have
to save my life thereby. For if I had feared death, I would not have come
hither to put my life in hazard: but prickt forward with spite and desire I
have to be revenged of them that thus have banished me." — II, 169–170.

[2] "Hereunto are also added the lives of Epaminondas, of Philip of Macedon, of Dionysius the elder, tyrant of Sicilia, of Augustus Caesar, of Plutarke, and of Seneca: with the lives of nine other excellent Chiefetaines of
warre: collected out of Aemylius Probus, by S. G. S. and Englished by the
aforesaid Translator." An account of the various editions is given in both
W. W. Skeat, *Shakespeare's Plutarch* (London, 1875), and C. F. Tucker
Boooke, work cited.

issued in 1612 and 1631; and in 1657, brief lives of twenty more "Eminent Persons," ancient and modern, from the French of Andrew Thevet, were added to the sixth edition. A seventh was published at Cambridge in 1676, but that was to be the last for more than two centuries. For in 1683 a new translation was made "by several hands," with the life of Plutarch "written by Mr. Dryden." Dryden's attitude to North's work is

first that it was but a Copy of a Copy, and that too but lamely taken from the Greek Original: Secondly that the English Language was then unpolish'd, and far from the perfection which it has since attain'd: So that the first Version is not only ungrammatical and ungraceful, but in many places almost unintelligible.[1]

The translation thus issued was itself superseded by that of the Langhornes (1770), who declared that "it was full of the grossest errors," and that its language "was insupportably tame, tedious, and embarrassed. The periods had no harmony; the phraseology had no elegance, no spirit, no precision." [2] The Langhornes do not mention North, they refer to his work as "the old English translation," and priding themselves on their vastly superior knowledge of Plutarch, they note that

it is said by those who are not willing to allow Shakespeare much learning, that he availed himself of the last-mentioned Translation; but they seem to forget that, in order to support their arguments of this kind, it is necessary for them to prove

[1] "The Epistle Dedicatory to His Grace the Duke of Ormond."
[2] In their preface.

that Plato too was translated into English at the same time; for the celebrated soliloquy, 'To be, or not to be' is taken almost verbatim from that Philosopher.[1]

North had descended into oblivion. A writer in the *Critical Review* for February, 1771, expressed the general opinion that his "was not a translation from Plutarch, nor can it be read with pleasure in the present age." Let us see then what could be read with pleasure:

When Caesar and Pompey had her favours, she was young and unexperienced; but she was to meet Antony at an age when beauty, in its full perfection, called in the maturity of the understanding to its aid. . . . Though she had received many pressing letters of invitation from Antony and his friends, she held him in such contempt, that she by no means took the most expeditious method of travelling. She sailed along the river Cydnus in a most magnificent galley. The stern was covered with gold, the sails were of purple, and the oars were silver. These, in their motion, kept time to the music of flutes, and pipes, and harps. The queen, in the dress and character of Venus, lay under a canopy embroidered with gold, of the most exquisite workmanship; while boys, like painted Cupids, stood fanning her on each side of the sopha. Her maids were of the most distinguished beauty, and, habited like the Nereids and the Graces, assisted in the steerage and conduct of the vessel. The fragrance of burning incense was diffused along the shores, which were covered with multitudes of people. Some followed the procession, and . . . numbers went down from the city to see it.[2]

Compared with this, the "tame and tedious" language of the so-called Dryden translation is a relief. Fortunately its phraseology had no eighteenth-century

---

[1] *Ibid.*

[2] J. Langhorne and W. Langhorne, *Plutarch's Lives* (London, 1770), V, 412–413.

pseudo-elegance; if it lacked distinction, it at least had vigor.[1] Clough recognized its superiority to the Langhornes' version when he published a revised edition in the middle of the last century.[2] But he does not seem even to have been aware of the existence of another translation. It remained for W. E. Henley and his associates to reinstate North as the English translator of Plutarch. Place either of the other [3] versions beside his, and you need nothing else to illustrate how great an art that of translation could be:

For Caesar and Pompey knew her when she was but a young thing, and knew not then what the worlde ment: but nowe she went to Antonius at the age when a womans beawtie

[1] "Their Acquaintance was with her when a Girle, young and ignorant in the Arts of Love, but she was now to meet Antony in the flower of her age with all the Charms of Beauty, and all the artifice of riper years. . . . Many were the Letters she received from Antony to hasten her coming, but she did not seem to make any great account of his Orders. At length she embarques upon a small Galley in the River Cydnus, the head of the Barge did shine with inlay'd Gold, the Sails were of Purple Silk, the Oares of Silver, which beat time to the Flutes and Hautbois, she herself lay all along under a Canopy of Cloth of Gold curiously imbroider'd, drest as Venus is ordinarily represented, and beautiful young Boys like Cupids stood on each side to fan her, her Maids were drest like Sea Nymphes and Graces, some steering the Rudder, some working at the Ropes, the perfumes diffus'd themselves from the Vessel to the Shore, which was all cover'd with multitudes meeting and following the Gally, all the People running out of the City to see this strange sight." — *Plutarch's Lives*, Translated from the Greek by Several Hands (London, 1683–1686); "The Life of Marcus Antonius," by Charles Frazer, M.D., V, 172–173.

[2] *Plutarch's Lives*, the translation called Dryden's, corrected from the Greek and revised by A. H. Clough (London, 1859).

[3] I naturally do not include in this comparison such a translation as that of Bernadotte Perrin for the Loeb Classical Library. It does not pretend to any independent literary existence, but simply to supplement the Greek text, for which purpose it is very useful.

is at the prime, and she also of best judgement. . . . Therefore when she was sent unto by divers letters, both from
Antonius him selfe, and also from his frendes, she made so
light of it, and mocked Antonius so much, that she disdained
to set forward otherwise, but to take her barge in the river of
Cydnus, the poope whereof was of gold, the sailes of purple,
and the owers of silver, which kept stroke in rowing after the
sounde of the musicke of flutes, howboyes, citherns, violls,
and such other instruments as they played upon in the barge.
And now for the person of her selfe: she was layed under a
pavillion of cloth of gold of tissue, apparelled and attired like
the goddesse Venus, commonly drawen in picture: and hard by
her, on either hand of her, pretie faire boyes apparelled as
painters doe set forth god Cupide, with little fannes in their
hands, with the which they fanned wind upon her. Her Ladies
and gentlewomen also, the fairest of them were apparelled
like the nymphes Nereides (which are the mermaides of the
waters) and like the Graces, some stearing the helme, others
tending the tackle and ropes of the barge, out of the which
there came a wonderfull passing sweete savor of perfumes,
that perfumed the wharfes side, pestered with innumerable
multitudes of people.   Some of them followed the barge all
alongest the rivers side: others also ranne out of the citie to
see her comming in.[1]

[1] VI, 25–26.

CHAPTER IV

Florio's Montaigne
(1603)

I

THE popularity and influence of Montaigne's *Essays* in England were immediate. Montaigne died in 1592, the definitive edition appeared in Paris in 1595, and on October 20 of the same year an entry in the Stationers' Register reads: "Edward Aggas entred for his copie under the handes of the Wardenes: 'The Essais of Michaell Lord Mountene.'" The wording would seem to indicate a translation, but of it no trace remains.

Whether or not this translation was executed, Montaigne was being widely read in England. Francis Bacon, whose brother Anthony had visited the essayist at Bordeaux, was quick to use this new literary form, and published his first volume of *Essays* in 1597. Between these two minds there is little kinship: Bacon, pithy, practical, and definite; Montaigne, genial, discursive, sceptical. But that Bacon had felt the force of Montaigne's example is evident from the fact that he coined the new word "essay" for his title. His one definite reference to Montaigne did not appear until the final edition of 1625, where, in the essay "Of Truth," to support his argument on the evils of lying, he wrote "Therefore Montaigne saith prettily," and followed it with a quotation from the essay "Du desmentir." And although both men treated the same subjects, "Of Parents and Children," "Of Custom and Education," "Of Death," and frequently filled their pages with similar general reflections,[1] both went back to a steady reading of the classics for their common source. However, the mere fact that a mind like Bacon's was drawn to the same subjects as Montaigne's had been, shows that England was ripe for such a book as *Les Essais*.

Its attractions were manifold. As a storehouse of quotations and illustrations from the classics, especially from Seneca and Plutarch, it satisfied the popular thirst for anecdotes and for sententious reflections on life. Its temper was fundamental for later Elizabethan England, since it expressed so many of the attitudes that were struggling for expression in her life and drama. Its moral ideal was strongly pagan: the normal harmony between body and soul. Montaigne, the sage eclectic, believed in a God "qui a créé les melons et les poissons . . . les bons vins du Médoc et les beaux corps de femmes." [2] Grace for him was not regeneration, but the natural aid which the feebleness of man found in the strength of God. Everything conforming to nature was good and divine.

[1] A number of interesting parallels are cited by A. H. Upham, *The French Influence in English Literature* (New York, 1911), pp. 524-528.

[2] P. Stapfer, *Montaigne* (Paris, 1895), p. 92.

Pagan symbols of Fortune, Destiny, and the gods meant as much to him as that of God. When he wished to illustrate the fact that Providence knows better than we what is good for us, he cited Juvenal, not Christ. Likewise his attitude toward death was purely pagan: death was something to be accepted without desire and without fear. Mortality appeared to him more clearly demonstrable than immortality; and the belief of his rich maturity was that man should give his efforts to learning, not how to die, but how to live.

Every phase of his broad philosophy struck some responsive note in England. The sane penetration of his scepticism was what her thinkers wanted, since it cleared their fevered minds and lifted from them the oppression of medieval authority. The chief attraction of the book probably lay in its full dramatic portrayal of an individual. This was a new quality in literature, and the force lying behind it, the rediscovery of man by himself, was the most fundamental and exciting factor in the English Renaissance. Samuel Daniel felt this force when he wrote his prefatory verses to Florio's translation of the *Essays*:

> And let the Critic say the worst he can,
> He can not say but that Montaigne yet
> Yeeldes most rich pieces and extracts of man;
> Though in a troubled frame confus'dly set.

Bacon was not alone in his quick reaction to Montaigne's form. In 1598, a certain Master Greeneham printed *Diverse Sermons and Tractes uppon severall Textes,* whose titles, "Of anger," "Of meditacon of deathe," "Of foolishness," again closely parallel Montaigne. Other writers followed in swift succession.[1] The popularity of the fashion is illustrated by the *Essays* of Sir William Cornwallis, 1600, which ran through half a dozen editions in thirty years. Cornwallis did not hesitate to assert his discipleship, cited his master frequently, wrote scarcely an essay which does not suggest him, and declared Montaigne

for profitable Recreation . . . most excellent. . . . In a word he hath made Morall Philosophy speake couragiously, and in steede of her gowne, given her an Armour; hee hath put Pedanticall Schollerisme out of countenance, and made manifest, that learning mingled with Nobilitie shines most clearly.[2]

This passage is of supreme interest since it shows the effect of Montaigne upon a characteristic Englishman, and illustrates the truth that a great book can be given as many interpretations as there are readers. Cornwallis

---

[1] Fritz Dieckow, *John Florio's Englische Übersetzung der Essais Montaigne's* (Strassburg, 1903), pp. 5–6, cites, among others, the following, taken from the Stationers' Register:

1601, 9 October: *Essayes,* by Master Robert Johnson (reissued 1607, 1610).

1608, 19 April: *Essayes politique and Morall to the right honorable the Lady Anne Harington.*

1608, 17 October: *Essaies Morall and Theologicall.*

1616, 10 June: *Essayes of certaine Paradoxes.*

1619, 13 September: *Essaies upon the five sences,* by Richard Brathwaite.

1620, 29 March: *A discourse against flattery and of Rome with Essaies.*

1621, 31 May: *A handfull of Essaies or Imperfect offers,* by William Mason.

[2] Essay XII, "Of Censuring."

caught from Montaigne the habit of random reflection
on every phase of existence, and he considered him great
because he had liberated moral philosophy from the
schools and had made it a vital part of the life of a
gentleman. His mental attitude was the reverse of his
master's: a serious Anglo-Saxon and the champion of
strict morality, he used the essay to state his positive
opinions. But this difference between them did not dim
his enthusiasm in the least. He had not read Montaigne
in the original, but

translated into a stile, admitting as few idle words as our language will endure. It is well fitted in this new garment, and
Montaigne speaks now good English. . . . It is done by a
fellow less beholding to nature for his fortune then witte, yet
lesser for his face then fortune; the truth is, he lookes more
like a good-fellow then a wise man, and yet hee is wise beyond
either his fortune or education.[1]

It is not certain whether this cryptic remark indicates
John Florio or one of the "seven or eight of great wit
and worth" whom the translator himself refers to so
glibly in the preface of his version as having "assayed,
but found these essayes no attempt for French appren-
tises." Florio's manuscript would have circulated freely
and Cornwallis may well have read it. And there is no
remark in his description that might not fit the translator. At all events the Stationers' Register had already
recorded on June 4, 1600, five months before the entry

[1] *Ibid.*

of Cornwallis' *Essays*: "The essais of Michell Lord of Montaigne translated into English by John Florio."

II

"Resolute John Florio,"[1] as he chose to sign his prefaces, had been a well-known figure in court circles many years before he dedicated his translation of Montaigne to six ladies of fashion. Leicester had been his first patron, Southampton had received him into his service, and on the accession of James I he was so much the most prominent of the group of gentleman instructors in Italian that his appointment as tutor to Prince Henry and reader to the Queen was almost a foregone conclusion. He had been well fitted by birth and early surroundings for his career as interpreter to Renaissance England of the languages and literatures of the Continent. His father, Michael Angelo Florio, was a Protestant minister who, to escape persecution, had fled with his family from Siena to England just before the accession of Edward VI. He became pastor to an Italian congregation in London, was patronized by Archbishop Cranmer, and resided in the house of Sir William Cecil. He was also a teacher, a writer on the education of children, and the author of a history of the life and death of Lady Jane Grey. But about the time of his son Gio-

---

[1] The fullest account of his career appears in Comtesse de Chambrun, *Giovanni Florio, Un Apôtre de la Renaissance en Angleterre à l'Epoque de Shakespeare* (Paris, 1921).

vanni's birth in 1553, the elder Florio was banished from Cecil's house on a charge of gross immorality, and he left England after the accession of Catholic Mary.

Consequently his son grew up abroad, whether in France or Italy is not certain. The exact date of his return to England is also unknown, but about 1576 John Florio was tutor in French and Italian to Emanuel Barnes, the son of the Bishop of Durham, a commoner at Magdalen College, Oxford. The elder Florio's disgrace had apparently been forgotten, for it seems never to have prevented his son's moving in the best society. According to Anthony à Wood, Florio himself matriculated at Magdalen in 1581 at the somewhat advanced age of twenty-eight, and "was a teacher and instructor of certain scholars in the university." But before that date he had printed his first book, in 1578, dedicating to the noble protection of Robert Dudley, Earl of Leicester:

Florio His firste Fruites: which yeelde familiar speech, merie Proverbes, wittie Sentences, and golden sayings.
Also a perfect Induction to the Italian, and English tongues, as in the Table appeareth.
The like heretofore, never by any man published.

The book is a bewildering assortment, as odd as its title. Some of the material is taken from Ariosto and the other Italian poets; but an indication of Florio's taste, as well as of his early linguistic activity, lies in the fact that a good third of the volume consists in a translation of Guevara into both Italian and English. His charming method of teaching the rudiments of a language, which recalls Erasmus' *Colloquies*, is by means of dialogues that display a lively picture of the country and its customs. Attractive settings are laid for these conversations,

> Methinkes we shal doo wel to syt downe here under the shadowe of these budded trees, and beginne to rehearse some fine Sentences, fine proverbs, and gentle sayeinges, made by some gentle Poete, and that commonly are used in the Italian language, and so we will passe awaye this greate heate.[1]

Although his English is sometimes awkward because it follows Italian constructions too closely,[2] nevertheless these short conversations in Florio's *First Fruites* carry you into the midst of Elizabethan England:

> What drinke do they drinke in Englande, wyne, or no? — No sir, they drinke beere, or els ale made of corne. — Which is best? know ye that? — To me beere seemeth best. — Is there no wine there? — Yes sir, and great plentie. — Whence comes it, out of France? — There cometh some from France, some from Spaine, & Candie. — What sortes of wine have they? — They have claret wine, red wine, Sacke, Muscadel, and Malmesey. — Is it deare or cheape? — Claret wine, red and white is sold for five pence the quart, and Sacke for sixe pence, Muscadel and Malmesey for eight. — It is not too deare. — No sir, but indifferent. . . .
>
> What pastime use they on holy dayes? — Of all sortes of pastyme, as Comedies, Tragedies, leaping, daunsing, playes

---

[1] Chap. 18.

[2] He calls foreign merchants "merchant strangers," through analogy with "mercanti stranieri"; and says, "The merchants are they loving?" ("Sono amabili"), when he means "Are they obliging?" Also "They get well" for "They make money" shows that he translated literally the idiom "Guadagno bene."

of defense, baiting of Beares, shooting in bowes, running, shooting in Gonnes, walking in the fields, going in boates upon the water.[1]

Or again, "What think you of the queene? — As for the queene, to tel you the plaine truth, no tongue is sufficient to praise her ynough." Then comes the customary heaping of adjectives, "She is learned, wise, gentle, curteous, noble, prudent, liberall, fayre, loving, vertuous; she is gallant, merciful and" — a great virtue in Florio's eyes — "speaketh al tongues." [2] But in spite of this eulogy, it becomes clear as the book progresses that his true purpose is not to make England known to Italians, but to show Englishmen the vast superiority of Italy, and instruct them how they should live. Their manners do not please him, and he gives his reasons:

What thinke you of the maners of English men? tel me of curtesie — I wyll tell you, some are well manered, but many yl. — Toward whom are they yl manered? — Toward Strangers: and fewe of these English men delight to have their chyldren learne divers languages, whiche thing displeaseth me. When I arrived first in London, I coulde not speake Englishe, and I met above five hundred persons, afore I coulde find one, that could tel me in Italian, or French, where the Post dwelt.[3]

No more does he conceal his dislike of certain of their practices, among others that the Italian rapier is not used universally, and that some still cling to their traditional defense: "What weapons beare they? — Some

---

[1] Chap. 15.   [2] Chap. 13.   [3] Chap. 27.

sword and dagger, some sword and buckler, a clownish dastardly weapon and not fit for a gentleman."

He so abhors levity that his reformer's tone is droll: "I would there were such a Lawe, that if one shold bring up his children without teachyng them somthing, & especially to reade, write, and speake divers languages, that he should be beheaded." A pretentious pedantry creeps out between the lines of this book. The tone is often pompous and affected, and Florio's first fruits are as green as the ten pieces of stumbling verse, in praise of the author, contributed to the book by his sometime students, among them the puritanical Stephen Gosson, author of *The School of Abuse*.

Two years later this extraordinary Italian master published a translation of Cartier's *Navigations*,[1] in the preface to which he urged the practicability of sending out "a sufficient number of men to plant a colonie in some convenient Haven" — one of the first times that such a daring suggestion had been made by a writer in English. Shortly afterwards he seems to have left the university for London life, since in 1583 he turns up in the service of the French ambassador, Michel de Castelnau.[2] He appears to have known all the celebrities of the

[1] *A short and Briefe Narration of the Two Navigations and Discoueries to the North-weast Partes called New Fraunce.* First translated out of French into Italian by that famous learned Man, Geo. Bapt. Ramutius, and now turned into English by John Florio, 1580.

[2] This fact has just been established by F. A. Yates, "John Florio at the French Embassy," *The Modern Language Review* (1929), XXIV, 16–36.

day. At the occasion of the meeting between Giordano
Bruno and Fulke Greville to discuss the Copernican
theory before a select audience, Florio and his friend Dr.
Matthew Gwinne,[1] a fellow of St. John's, escorted the
distinguished visitor to the banquet. Bruno has left the
account,[2] in one of the most living of all surviving pictures of the Elizabethan day, of how they started out
in a boat on the Thames, and how Florio sang "come
ricordandosi de' suoi amori," the philosopher joining in
the refrains. But the conclusion of their trip was less
romantic. The boatman suddenly put ashore and refused to go any farther, although they were only oppo-
site the Temple. So they were forced to struggle up the
bank knee-deep in mud, and stumbled through the dark
until they at last came out on the Strand, "la grande ed
ordinaria strada" — not a stone's throw from where
they had started. When they finally reached their des-
tination, after a whole series of similar vicissitudes, the
other guests were already seated. One of Bruno's party
— it seems to have been Florio — was offered the least
honorable place, but declined it with humble politeness,

[1] Matthew Gwinne, M.D. (1558?-1627), had an interesting career. He
was for a time (1582-83) lecturer in Music at St. John's, Oxford, and later
appointed to oversee and provide for the plays at Christ Church. He wrote
a Latin play to be presented at Magdalen at the time of the visit of James to
Oxford in 1605, which pleased the King but did not keep him awake. At the
founding of Gresham College, London, he was the first Professor of Physic.
He often supported the position that the frequent use of tobacco was beneficial.

[2] *La Cena de le Ceneri*, "Dialogo Secondo," 1584 (ed. Milan, 1864), p. 43.

mistaking it for the head of the table, and tried instead to take the place of honor. From then on the figure of the translator is forgotten in the blazing violence of Bruno's triumph over the learned company, which finally causes the evening to break up in confusion.

It is not certain how long Florio remained with the embassy after Castelnau's return to France in 1585; but whatever he did, he contrived to stay in favor with the great. For when, in 1598, he dedicated his *Worlde of Wordes* to the "most noble, most vertuous, and most Honorable Earle of Southampton," he said that he had lived "some yeeres" in his lordship's "paie and patronage," and owed and vowed to him the years that were to come. Shakespeare dedicated *Venus and Adonis* to Southampton in 1593, and *Lucrece* in the following year, so that the poet and the Italian master seem to have interested the wealthy young lord at about the same time; and their own acquaintance probably starts from this date. But somewhat earlier Florio had issued his *Second Frutes, To be gathered of twelve Trees of divers but delightsome tastes to the tongues of Italians and Englishmen. To which is annexed his Gardine of Recreation, yeelding six thousand Italian Proverbs (1591)*.

Here the tone is much mellower than in *Firste Fruites*. Florio is still the violent champion of Italian, and against the saying, "Un Inglese italianato è un Diavolo incarnato," which Ascham had used in *The Scholemaster*, he storms: "Now who the Divell taught thee so much

Italian? speake me as much more and take all. . . . Mis-
like you the language? Why the best speake it best and
hir Majestie none better." [1] But he no longer despises
the country of his adoption, and his conversations flow
lightly around the theatre, horses, food and drink, skill
in fencing, the way to travel, gaming and chess. In the
second chapter a dialogue commences between Master
John and one of his pupils named Henry (not impossibly Henry Wriothesley): "What shall wee doo untill it
be dinner time? — Let us make a match at tennis. —
Agreed, this coole morning calls for it. — And then after
dinner we will goe see a plaie." [2] Nor is humor lacking,
for in the conversation where Florio collected all the
words necessary to be known for a banquet, he wrote:
"Ile give you none of this goose, for she is too hard. —
Is it not that which saved the Romanes Capitoll? —
Nay I thinke she was rather her great grandmother.
— Or rather to that which entered Noës Arke." [3]

In the preface to *Second Frutes* Florio promised that
he would shortly send forth "an exquisite Italian and
English dictionary." This *Worlde of Wordes*, printed in
triple columns in thick folio, and embracing 46,000
words, was not finished for seven years. Then it appeared in grand style, dedicated to three of his pupils —
he could have selected none more notable — the Earl of
Rutland, the Earl of Southampton, and the Countess of
Bedford, to all of whom he gave high and varied praise

---

[1] "To the Reader."   [2] p. 23.   [3] p. 61.

for their skill in Italian. The countess was later to stand him in good stead. At the time of the Essex conspiracy, when Southampton was sent to the Tower and Florio was left without support, he was received into the household of her mother, Lady Anne Harington, a cousin by marriage of Sir John Harington, the translator of Ariosto. Here it was, as he relates in his "Epistle Dedicatorie," that at the charge of Sir Edward Wotton he undertook the translation of one of Montaigne's essays, and that Lady Harington, having read it, urged him on.

The translation thus begun, and not finally given to the world until three years after its entry in the Stationers' Register, eclipsed in splendor all of Florio's previous efforts. He could not be content to dedicate this magnificent folio to any less than a galaxy of six ladies of the court. The first book is, of course, for the Countess of Bedford and her mother. The second is divided between Lady Penelope Rich, Sidney's *Stella*, and his daughter Elizabeth, Countess of Rutland, with an appropriate eulogy of the "perfect-unperfect" *Arcadia*. The third is given gracefully to two of Florio's younger pupils, Lady Elizabeth Grey, daughter of the Earl of Shrewsbury, and Lady Mary Nevill, daughter of England's Lord High Treasurer. The volume is further embellished by sonnets to the various ladies from Dr. Gwinne, under the name "Il Candido"; [1] by an Italian

---

[1] That "Il Candido" refers to Dr. Gwinne is made most probable by W. C. Hazlitt's entry, concerning the *Worlde of Wordes*, in his *Collections and*

sonnet from the same, "Al mio amato Instruttore Mr. Giovanni Florio;" and by a long poem, "To my deere friend . . . concerning his translation of Montaigne," by the well-known Samuel Daniel.

What made Florio consider Montaigne worthy of being translated were his "so pleasing passages, so judicious discourses, so delightsome varieties, so persuasive conclusions, such learning of all sortes, and above all, so elegant a French style."[1] He confesses him "odcrotcheted," extravagant, scattered, and paradoxical, but he does not think that "such extraordinarinesse" ever displeases readers, especially not when it comes from him whose just title is "Sole Maister of Essayes." No pains, he feels, can be misspent in making known to Englishmen so rare and eminent an author. Florio does not exaggerate the importance of the art of translation, but neither does he fail to appreciate fully the extent of his own labors. He admits the objection against all translation that "the sense may keepe form; the sentence is disfigured; the fineness, fitnesse, featenesse diminished: as much as artes nature is short of natures arte, a picture of a body, a shadow of a substance."[2] Some, he says, may bring the charge against him that

Notes (London, 1876), p. 162: "At the end of the first sonnet by 'Il Candido' occurs in an extant copy the following MS note in a coeval hand: 'Gwin his name was, which in Wellsh signifieth white, and therefore calleth himselfe il Candido, which is white in Italian.'"

[1] The dedication to the second book.
[2] "To the curteous Reader."

he has "made of good French no good English," [1] but his reply to all critics is that if the errors are of matter they are the author's; if of omission, the printer's. "If any thinke he could do better, let him trie; then will he better thinke of what is done." [1] In the completion of his work he acknowledges the help of Theodore Diodati,[2] the father of Milton's friend, with whom he conferred constantly, and who has been to him "in this rough-rockie Ocean" like "a guide-fish to the Whale." [3] His "onelie dearest and in love-sympathising friend," Master Doctor Gwinne, had undertaken the vast task of tracing to their sources all the quotations from the classics, since to Florio's pedantic soul the way in which Montaigne had thrown these in at random constituted his greatest blemish. Upheld and armed by these two supporters of knowledge and friendship, the translator has "passt the pikes," and is able to strike an attitude: "I sweat, I wept, and I went on, til now I stand at bay." And whatever his readers may find fault with, he will remain "still resolute John Florio."

III

In *Firste Fruites* Florio had given utterance to an opinion of English reminiscent of the mid-sixteenth-century dissatisfaction with the language:

[1] "To the curteous Reader."

[2] Theodore Diodati (*c.* 1574–1650) was a brother of Giovanni Diodati, the distinguished Geneva divine. Himself a doctor and a graduate of the University of Leyden, he attended Prince Henry and Princess Elizabeth.

[3] "The Epistle Dedicatorie."

It doth not like me at al, because it is a language confused,
bepeesed with many tongues: it taketh many words of the
latine, & mo from the French, & mo from the Italian, and
many mo from the Dutch, some also from the Greeke & from
the Britaine, so that if every language had his owne wordes
againe, there would but a fewe remaine for Englishmen, and
yet every day they adde. Take a book and reade, but marke
well, and you shall not reade foure woordes together of true
English.[1]

This is the tone of Thomas Wilson's famous objection to
"any strange inkehorne termes"; but whether Florio's
criticisms are anything more than affectation is doubtful in view of his remark, in the preface to the *Worlde of
Wordes*, that English gentlemen must take pleasure in
finding so rich a tongue as the Italian outvied by their
mother-speech "as by the manie-folde Englishes of
manie wordes in this is manifest." Still more doubtful
does the sincerity of his earlier strictures become when
he decribes himself to Lady Harington as the foster-
father of Montaigne's work, "having transported it
from France to England; put it in English clothes;
taught it to talke our tongue (though many-times with
a jerke of the French jargon)." [2]

He is now in accord with the trend that produced the
vast enrichment of the Elizabethan tongue. He believes
there are many likely French words that, by being
coupled with common words to explain them, may be
made "familiar with our English, which well may beare

---

[1] Chap. 27.
[2] "The Epistle Dedicatorie."

them." [1] He cites a number of such words, which he says some critics may object to: "entraine, conscientious,[2] endeare, tarnish, comporte, efface, facilitate, ammusing, debauching, regret, effort, emotion." And these, even more than the "hard words" of which Crispinus is medically relieved in the last scene of *The Poetaster*, fit easily into our modern vocabulary, and bear out the soundness of Florio's practice.[3]

---

[1] "To the curteous Reader."

[2] The *New English Dictionary* gives Cotgrave, 1611, for the first appearance in the language of "conscientious."

[3] In other cases Florio's borrowed words have either disappeared, or are no longer in general use. For example:

Borrowed	Usual
accommodable	suitable
allegations	quotations
arrest (Fr. *arrêt*)	decree
bonifie (Fr. *bonifier*)	to do a kindness
bransles	movements
bruites	noises
calepine	dictionary
cautelous (Fr. *cauteleux*)	artful
debonarity (Fr. *débonnaireté*)	courtesy
debordement	disorder
defeate (Fr. *défaite*)	evasion
deffailance (Fr. *défaillance*)	languor
demisextiers (Fr. *demi-setier*)	half-pints
devoir	duty
dissemblable	dissimilar
enterparly (Fr. *entreparler*)	negotiate
gaillardise	indiscretion
gests	deeds
inutile	useless
jovissance (Fr. *jouissance*)	enjoyment
liminary (Fr. *liminaire*)	dedicatory
male (Fr. *malle*)	trunk
maquorelage (Fr. *maquerellage*)	seduction

The first thing that strikes the reader of his translation is his passionate delight in words. Speaking of
those who voluntarily mortify the flesh, Montaigne had
written: "J'en ay veu engloutir du sable, de la cendre,
& se travailler à point nommé de ruiner leur estomac,
pour acquerir les pasles couleurs." [1] And Florio translates: "I have seen some swallow gravell, ashes, *coales*,
dust, *tallow*, *candles*, and for the-nonce, labour and *toyle*
themselves to spoile their stomacke, only to get a pale-
bleake colour." [2] He takes an abandoned joy in elaborating. He loves what is, to him, a fine excess. Montaigne
is talking of his servants: "Je ne voy rien autour de moy
que couvert & masqué," [3] and Florio plunges ahead with
"I see nothing about me, but *inscrutable hearts*, *hollow
mindes*, fained *looks*, dissembled *speeches*, and *counter-
feit actions*." [4]

Sometimes he puts in additional words in the attempt
to heighten the situation by emphasis. Such expressions

outrecuidance	arrogance
paillardize (Fr. *paillardise*)	lewdness
preallable (Fr. *préalable*)	preliminary
preud'hommie	sincerity
semblable	similar
sortable	suitable
tintimare (Fr. *tintamarre*)	a great din

[1] Montaigne, *Les Essais*, ed. E. Courbet and Ch. Royer (Paris, 1872), I,
339. All page references are to this edition.
[2] Florio, *Montaigne*, Tudor Translations, ed. G. Saintsbury (London,
1892), I, 285. All page references are to this edition.
[3] I, 365.
[4] I, 308.

as "these *boistrous* billows" [1] for "ces flots," [2] "*lowring* vexation and *drooping* melancholy" [3] for "le chagrin & la melancholie," [4] "the *minde-quelling* authoritie of his countenance, and *awe-moving* fiercenesse of his words" [5] for "l'autorité de son visage & la fierté de ses paroles," [6] suggest through their adjectives a strained emotional pitch quite foreign to Montaigne. Sometimes qualifying words are inserted simply through the desire for adornment, as in "It is no historie to be *fabulously* reported, but a historie to be *dutifully* reverenced, *awfully* feared, and *religiously* adored," [7] where all these adverbs are lacking in the original.[8]   Sometimes a word is added which throws the meaning into more vivid relief: an adverb for greater precision ("who *expresly* forbade" [9] for "qui deffendit"[10]), verbs that are more significant ("to manage a horse, *to tosse* a pike, *to shoot-off a peece*, *to play* upon the lute or *to warble* with the voice" [11] for "à manier un cheval, ou une pique, ou une lute, ou la voix" [12]). But often the reason for the addition is the sheer love of words for words' sake, since no new quality whatever is brought to the meaning. On occasion two nouns become seven: "contract & testament" [13] are swollen to "*law-cases, bils*, contracts, *indentures, citations, wils* and testaments." [14]   Thus, frequently, Montaigne's strength is lost in a choking mass.

[1] II, 131.	[2] II, 152.	[3] II, 283.	[4] II, 326.
[5] I, 130.	[6] I, 154.	[7] I, 369.	[8] I, 439.
[9] I, 27.	[10] I, 20.	[11] I, 158.	[12] I, 185.
[13] IV, 210.	[14] III, 330.		

The affinities of Florio's style are quickly manifest. In his love of doubling he suggests euphuism, but another influence is far more definite. At this time the vogue in England of the Huguenot poet Du Bartas (1544-90) was overwhelming.[1] An avowed follower of Ronsard, he had taken from him the freedom of inventing compounds, and had developed it at random [2] in his three Biblical epics, *Judith*, *La Semaine* (the story of the Creation), and *La Seconde Semaine* (the story of mankind). These are fluent, irrepressible, and ill-regulated volumes of metrical ingenuity. With no faculty of selection on their author's part, Du Bartas' epics became crude encyclopedias of science. But they throbbed with vigorous natural description, boundless enthusiasm for the splashing of a waterfall or the points of a horse, and above all, with a constant turbulent surge of action.

In France their popularity flared and went out like a comet; in England it shone for a century, a weird fixed star. This is an illustration of the same principle that accounts for Byron's lingering popularity on the Continent and for Victor Hugo's being in America still frequently called a great novelist. A people speaking a different tongue are often not so sensitive to a writer's excesses or limitations, and find in his rhetoric an expression of

[1] I am indebted here to Upham, pp. 145-218, and to Lee, *The French Renaissance in England*, pp. 333-355.

[2] He describes fire as:
"Le feu donne-clarté, porte-chaud, jette-flamme
Source de mouvement, chasse-ordure, donne-âme."

elemental force. The Elizabethans seized on Du Bartas with ardor, for he gave articulation to their love of extravagant speech and daring compounds, and contained a suggestion of the dramatic that stirred their blood.

James VI of Scotland had been an early admirer; swept away by his enthusiasm he had sent a letter, mentioning the relationship of Alexander and Diogenes, and begging the poet to come to visit him. Du Bartas came in 1587, stayed several months, and continued his journey in triumph to England, where he was received by Elizabeth. Sidney translated a portion of *The First Week*. Gabriel Harvey gave Du Bartas a place beside Dante for elevation and majesty, and called Euripides his inferior.[1] The more sober Spenser, in a passage in *The Ruins of Rome*, ranked him with Du Bellay. Drayton declared that wrackful time should have no power to waste his "courtly French." [2] Lodge thought him as delightful as any author in Latin or Greek who had ever written of God and His works.[3] Even Donne seems to have felt his power.

Florio was caught in the full force of this excitement. Speaking of Sidney's translation, in his dedication to the second book of the *Essays*, he refers to Du Bartas as

[1] Harvey, *Works*, II, 103.

[2] In the dedication of his poem "Moyses in a Map of his Miracles" (1604) to Du Bartas and Sylvester.

[3] Lodge's last literary work was *A Learned Summarie upon the famous Poeme of William of Saluste, Lord of Bartas*, translated out of [Goulart's] French (1621).

"that arch-poet." He had without doubt also read
Joshua Sylvester's version, which was loyal to all the
French poet's tricks of style, and especially to the compound epithet. How profoundly Florio felt the influence
can be read on every page of his Montaigne. We have
already seen how he shared the Elizabethan desire for
energy and movement and how it caused him to heap up
words. His love of compounds is just as great. "L'âme
pleine" [1] becomes "a mind full-fraught," [2] and the language of Philippe de Commines, which Montaigne had
called "doux & aggreable," [3] is "a pleasing-sweet and
gently-gliding speech." [4] Words are combined in almost
every fashion, and often with an extraordinarily fine
effect; for example, "marble-hearted," [5] coming upon
which, in Lear's speech to Goneril, one would have
thought it a certain stroke of Shakespeare's genius.[6] A
suggestion of the stage lies in the substitution of the
phrase "with a faint-trembling voyce and selfe-accusing
looke" [7] for the simple "d'une voix tremblante"; [8] and
the note of the sonnet cycles is caught in "pride-puft
majestie," [1] "the fresh-bleeding memorie," [9] and "with
high-swelling and heaven-disimbowelling words." [10] In

---

[1] I, 166.   [2] I, 140.   [3] II, 124.   [4] II, 108.

[5] "so marble-hearted and savage-minded men," II, 123, for "des âmes
si farouches," II, 141.

[6] "Ingratitude! thou marble-hearted fiend," *Lear*, I, iv.

[7] I, 182. In every instance Montaigne had written in strict simplicity:
"la maiesté si enflée," I, 193; "la recente memoire," I, 387; "enfle des mots,"
I, 211.

[8] I, 123.   [9] I, 146.   [10] I, 325.

many cases Florio's combinations possess a substantial richness, as in "a rough-hewen fellow"[1] for "un grossier,"[2] or "a lingering-toylsome life"[3] for "une vie peneuse."[3] As could have been expected, Florio's enthusiasm also carries him into the popular Elizabethan excess of compounding with no addition to the sense. "Filching-theft"[4] and "long-long discourses"[5] bring nothing to the simple word, and "the close-smacking, sweetnesse-moving, love-alluring, and greedie-smirking kisses of youth"[6] utterly destroys the rhythm and intensity of "les estroits baisers de la jeunesse, savoreux, gloutons, et gluans."[7]

Among the figures of the euphuistic style[8] Florio makes the greatest use of doubling, to gain the rhetorical ornament of successive phrases or clauses of approximately equal length. Sometimes the balance is attained between the two members by filling out one or both of them with adjectives: "not only prove *faint and* cold friends, but *cruell and sharpe* enemies"[9] for "les rende non froids amis seulement, mais ennemis."[10] However, Florio does not confine himself to such slight changes, but doubles whole phrases: "in the flowre of his growth *and spring of his youth*"[11] for "dans la fleur de son croist,"[12] "the *confused noise of warre and* clangor of

---

[1] I, 220.   [2] I, 256.   [3] II, 34.   [4] I, 149.
[5] I, 177.   [6] I, 364.   [7] I, 432.
[8] M. W. Croll gives an excellent definition of the chief characteristics of euphuism in his introduction to *Euphues*, pp. xv–xvi.
[9] I, 60.   [10] I, 68.   [11] I, 71.   [12] I, 82.

armes"[1] for "le bruit des armes."[2] Furthermore, he doubles the image or idea. Out of Montaigne's "Il n'est que de siffler en paume, je leur iray fournir des Essays, en chair et en os,"[3] he makes "They neede but *hold up their hand, or* whistle in their fiste, and I will store them with Essayes, of pithe and substance, *with might and maine*."[4] The last part of this sentence serves as an example of how Florio's flowing style can completely obscure a vivid point. Usually, however, he doubles an image with extraordinary felicity. "A groome or a horse-keeper may finde an hour to thrive in; *and a dog hath a day*"[5] is his rendering for "Ce n'est pas à dire que le muletier n'y trouve son heure."[6] And to the French proverb "d'avoir trouvé la fève au gasteau"[7] he adds the English "*to have hit the naile on the head, or* to have found out the beane of this Cake."[8]

Not infrequently, as in these last instances, Florio seems to have used doubling for a double purpose: to decorate his style, and to make the meaning fuller for his English reader. Here he has suggested a native proverb alongside the foreign one. He elsewhere fulfills the intention stated in his preface of linking a common word with one from the French which the English language might well bear: "received him into grace and favour"[9] ("le reçeut en grace,"[10]) "ruth or pitie"[11]

[1] III, 19. [2] III, 259. [3] III, 317. [4] III, 65.
[5] II, 8.   [6] II, 5.   [7] II, 257.   [8] II, 223.
[9] I, 14.   [10] I, 4.   [11] I, 17.

("pitié," [1]) "paine and care" [2] ("peine," [3]) "sorceries and witchcrafts" [4] ("sorcelleries," [5]) "Of Praiers and Orisons" [6] ("Des prieres," [7]) "urging and provoking them" [8] ("les provoquans," [1]) "advised and resolved themselves" [9] ("s'adviserent" [10]). In most of these cases the word from Montaigne had been introduced into English long before. But Florio's feeling that it might be unfamiliar to his readers is certainly a strong factor in causing many of his doublets. When this factor is not present, the doublets generally blur the voice of Montaigne in rhetoric, as in such a fatuous sentence as, "The Gods have rather placed *labour and* sweat at the entrances, *which lead* to Venus chambers, than *at the doores, that direct* to Pallas cabinets," [11] instead of the pointed "Les Dieux ont mis plustost la sueur aux advenues des cabinetz de Venus que de Pallas." [12]

Florio also shares Euphues' love of alliteration. "Carke and care," [13] "pricke and praise," [14] "bounds and barres," [15] "so fained and fond a ceremonie," [16] "tedious and mind-trying idlenesse," [17] and the more elaborate "Being absent I ... should lesse feele the ruinous downe-fall of a Towne, than being present, the fall of a

---

[1] I, 8. [2] I, 84. [3] I, 98. [4] I, 94.
[5] I, 109. [6] I, 365. The title of Essay LVI.
[7] I, 434. [8] I, 17. [9] I, 14. [10] I, 4.
[11] I, 171. [12] I, 198. [13] I, 84 ("de nous peiner," I, 98).
[14] II, 41 ("la palme," II, 43).
[15] I, 18 ("les barriers," I, 10).
[16] I, 23 ("une si feinte ceremonie," I, 16).
[17] I, 258 ("oisiveté ennuyeuse," I, 306).

Tile " [1] — all creep into the text without a hint from the French. He extends his use of alliteration to the favorite euphuistic trick of contrasting two words of about the same sound but with different meaning as, "could we as well enfold, as we can unfold our consideration." [2] The device of giving a similar sound to the two members of a series also appears often: "with such indiscreet impatience and impatient indiscretion," [3] "the more nicely close and closely nice it is." [4] Nor does Florio hesitate to extend the meaning if by so doing he can gain a rhetorical figure, and where Montaigne had simply denoted a tutor who kept a pupil from following his own tastes as "si fol," [5] the translator pronounces him "so foolishly-severe or so severely froward." [6]

It is easy to explain all Florio's tricks and ornaments of style. They simply show him moving in accordance with some of the tendencies of late sixteenth-century prose, and influenced by the then popular manner of expression. That this manner was remote from Montaigne's did not bother his contemporaries, for Florio

---

[1] III, 195. "Towne" is an obvious misprint for "Tower" ("Absent, je . . . sentirois moins lors la ruyne d'une tour, que je ne fais present, la cheute d'une ardoyse," IV, 54).

[2] II, 79 ("si nous sçavions replier aussi bien qu'estendre nostre consideration," II, 89). This is one of the instances where Florio's meaning is difficult for modern readers, owing partly to his literal rendering of the French "consideration." Cotton's version reads, "could we but apply our observation to our own concerns, as well as extend it to others."

[3] II, 42 ("avec tant d'indiscretion & d'impatience," II, 44).

[4] III, 109 ("plus mineuse & couverte," III, 368).

[5] I, 217.　　　　　　　　　　　　　[6] I, 188.

gave them the *Essays* in a form they were accustomed to and liked. And as long as the writings of Lyly and Du Bartas were still living forces, readers did not mind the artificiality of the one or the extravagance of the other any more than they objected to these things forty years ago in Pater and Swinburne. The essential thing for Florio was to make Montaigne vital to Englishmen. He achieved his end, partly in spite of, partly on account of, his departures from his original, but mainly because the Zeitgeist breathed through him, and he was able to translate Montaigne's freshness and vigor into native terms. To turn from his use of words and the details of his style to a consideration of larger units will suggest how, with all his differences from his author, he contrived to keep the essential spirit of the book.

IV

It will clear the ground for a more general discussion of Florio's qualities to dispose first of his obvious mistakes. His punctuation is chaotic, any number of single words are left out, negatives appear for positives, and singulars for plurals on nearly every page. To be sure he had provided for such slips by the nonchalant statement in his preface that the "Printers wanting a diligent Corrector, my many employments, and the distance betweene me and my friends I should conferre-with, may extenuate, if not excuse, even more errors." [1] At

---

[1] "To the curteous Reader."

the door of the printer may be laid at least some of the many mistakes in spelling which gave an amusingly wrong word: "societie" [1] as a rendering for "satiété," [2] "light" [3] for "nuict," [4] "infancie" [5] for "infamie," [6] "ill favour" [7] for "mauvaise senteur," [8] and "it vanisheth in the first moneth" [9] for "en la première bouche." [10] Others are doubtless due to "the falsenesse of the French prints." For instance, when Florio wrote "Some vices I shun; but othersome I eschew" [11] as a translation for "Je suy quelques vices: mais j'en fuy d'autres," [12] he obviously read "fuy" for both.

It may be remarked that in this last case Florio ought to have known he was writing nonsense. But when one examines the mistakes that cannot possibly be blamed on the printer, it becomes evident that the translator wrote at full speed, with little reflection, and no reconsideration of his result. He trips over himself in his haste: "Why shall I not judge of Alexander, as I am sitting and drinking at table," [13] is what he gives for "Pourquoi ne jugeray-je d'Alexandre à table devisant

---

[1] I, 72.   [2] I, 84.   [3] I, 208.
[4] I, 241.   [5] II, 11.   [6] II, 7.
[7] I, 111.   [8] I, 130.   [9] III, 279.

[10] IV, 149. Printer's errors are more numerous in the second (1613) edition than in the first (1603), and far more numerous in the third (1632) than in the second. This fact is clearly shown by the careful collation of the three texts made by A. R. Waller for the Temple Classics edition of the *Essays* (London, 1897), and from F. Dieckow's analysis, work cited, pp. 49–55. Consequently the use of the 1632 text for the Tudor Translation reprint was most unfortunate.

[11] II, 118.   [12] II, 137.   [13] I, 350.

et beuvant?" [1] When he comes to the name of Aristotle, he follows it with Plato,[2] not stopping to observe that Montaigne had written "Cato." [3] Often he just reverses the sense, as in stating that "no man should blame us for anything we doe against our conscience." [4] He frequently loses the meaning by clumsiness, and at other times succeeds in making it curiously confused, as when he renders "Car comme le monde se voit party, pour trois belles, il nous en faut baiser cinquante laides" [5] by "For as the world is divided into foure parts, so for foure faire ones we must kiss fiftie foule." [6] Throughout his translation Florio's numbers are thus blithely inaccurate, sometimes owing to his love of fullness, as in the substitution of "And how many have we seene die when they have had a whole Colledge of Physitians round about their bed, and looking in their excrements" [7] for the more sober "ayants trois medecins à leur cul." [8] But usually the inaccuracy is mere hurried disregard, since he obviously did not consider such details to be important.[9]

[1] I, 414. [2] III, 299.

[3] "ny Aristote ny Caton," IV, 173.

[4] I, 60 (Montaigne, I, 67). Another instance occurs where Montaigne was speaking of the Sea-Hares in India, "so that we die, if we but touch them," II, 324, instead of "de maniere que du seul attouchement nous les tuons," II, 373.

[5] III, 370. [6] III, 110. [7] III, 358. [8] IV, 242.

[9] Other examples are numerous: "after he hath there spent ten or twelve yeeres," I, 140, for "après quinze ou seize ans," I, 166; "a Bretton of three-score yeeres of age," III, 354, for "un Breton de soixante dix ans," IV, 238; "I was married at thirty yeares of age," II, 72, for "Je me mariay à trente trois ans." II, 81. This last is important since it refers to Montaigne himself.

But Florio's most astonishing mistakes are not his
downright inaccuracies, nor are they the many passages
where he follows the French too closely, nor those where
he annihilates the meaning by a random addition or by
applying his tricks of style without having first grasped
the sense. For sometimes he confuses the most simple
French words, and, although there may have been a
misprint in his text, a monent's pause would have shown
him his error. But that moment the Elizabethan Lon-
doners do not seem to have possessed any more than the
twentieth-century New Yorkers; and so Florio writes
"he framed the presumptuous over-weening of Nem-
broth,"[1] where the sense obviously demands "struck,"
and where he mixes "battre" with "batir." By a happy
chance the reading of "baiser" ("to kiss"), instead of
"baisser" ("to turn down"), does not render the account of a Roman custom too fantastic: "In Rome it was
heretofore a signe of favor to wring and kisse the
thumbs"[2] ("de comprimer et baisser"[3]). But in the
essay, "Of Moderation," the substitution of a diet of
"poison" for "fish" makes the humor more damag-
ing;[4] and in view of Florio's own love of word-play, it is
curious to see him miss one of Montaigne's and give for
"autant soigneuse d'en esteindre l'une, que d'estendre

[1] II, 270.   [2] II, 427.
[3] III, 100.
[4] "He to whom poison should be more healthy than meat," I, 216, for
"à qui le poisson seroit plus appetissant que la chair," I, 251.

l'autre" [1] the flat "to be as carefull to extinguish the
one, as diligent to quench the other." [2]

When the mistakes of Florio's three volumes are set
down in as many pages they suggest a mass of confusion
which does not exist. For with the exception of a certain
irritation at his diffuseness and bombast, and a difficulty in following some of his swollen sentences to their
conclusion, Florio's reader moves fairly smoothly
through the *Essays*. He might move with even more delight if he were aware of what pains the translator took
to make his path more easy. Florio always considered
it his duty to explain any terms he thought might be
difficult, and frequently to instruct his readers in details
that Montaigne had left to their discretion. We have
already seen his device for making clear the meaning of
a word from the French.[3] He also helps the Englishman
to understand the references to foreign history. "Le
Duc de Valentinois," [4] "le feu Chancelier Olivier," [5]
and "Solyman" [6] are all given a word of explanation,
thus: "Caesar Borgia, Duke of Valentinois," [7] "Lord
Oliver, whilome Chaunceler of France," [8] and "Soliman,
the great Turke." [9] "L'Ostracisme et le Petalisme" [10]
are translated as "the Ostracisme amongst the Athen-
ians, and the Petalisme among the Siracusans." [11] Even

---

[1] IV, 275.   [2] III, 387.
[3] As in "the Magazin of Memorie . . . the store-house of Invention," I,
42, for "le magasin de la memoire . . . celuy de l'invention," I, 42.
[4] I, 278.   [5] III, 38.   [6] III, 95.   [7] I, 236.
[8] II, 380.   [9] II, 423.   [10] III, 150.   [11] II, 466.

"le Louvre" [1] is given a note: "Louvre, the pallace of our Kings in Paris." [2]

Florio explains many French terms by putting the English equivalents beside them. Montaigne believed that a man who had something to say could always express it, "soit en Bergamasque." [3] To this Florio adds "although it be in Bergamask, or Welsh." [4] When he comes to "comediens qui le valent," [5] he brings it into more popular usage by saying: "good and honest Comedians, or (as we call them) Players." [6] Learned words, the vocabularies of medicine and philosophy, are his delight — or that of the two doctors who assisted him. "La phthysie" [7] is explained as "a Phthysique or consumption of the lungs," [8] "hydrophorbie" [9] as "hydrophobia or feare of waters," [10] "la dysenterie" [7] as "a dysentery or bloody flix." [8] But his most masterful definition occurs where Montaigne mentioned "l'endroit du diaphragme": [11] "Diaphragma, which is a membrane lying overthwart the lower part of the breast, separating the heart and lights from the stomache." [12]

In all these instances, as when "entelechy" [13] is made clear to the general public as "entelechy, or perfection moving of itselfe," [14] Florio is really giving footnotes, although he incorporates them in his text. The "Theatre

---

[1] IV, 114.   [2] III, 249.   [3] I, 209.
[4] I, 180.   [5] I, 219.   [6] I, 190.
[7] IV, 174.   [8] III, 299.   [9] II, 306.
[10] II, 266.   [11] III, 114.   [12] II, 437.
[13] II, 295.   [14] II, 256.

aux arenes"[1] is "so called in French because it is full of sand."[2] Even when his words run riot, his purpose is substantially that of a modern editor. For example, he wants to explain the ceremony that made Montaigne an honorary Roman citizen. He thinks that "une bulle authentique de bourgeoisie Romaine: qui me fut octroyée dernierement que j'y estois, pompeuse en seaux, & lettres dorées"[3] needs a little elaboration. With this purpose he renders it (adding, incidentally, uncalled-for trimmings of his own): "an authenticke Bull, *charter or patent* of *denizonship or* borgeouship of Rome, which at my last being there, was granted me *by the whole Senate of that Citie:* garish *and trimly adorned with goodly* Seales, and *written* in *faire* golden letters."[4]

But Florio's notes are sometimes purely gratuitous, as when he clarifies the meaning of a Greek term which Montaigne had not even used. "Ceci ne touche pas les centons,"[5] Montaigne had declared at the opening of his discussion of education, but Florio goes him more than one better with: "This concerneth not those minglemangles of many kinds of stuffe, or as the Grecians call them Rapsodies."[6] His sheer joy in elaborating every detail of a situation quite clear in the original appears in his version of the story (illustrating the force of imagination) of Marie Germain, an old man who had thought he was a girl until he was twenty-two years old:

[1] I, 60. [2] I, 55. [3] IV, 118.
[4] III, 253. [5] I, 179. [6] I, 151.

Faisant, dit-il, quelque effort en saultant, ses membres virils se produisirent: & est encore en usage entre les filles de là, une chanson, par laquelle elles s'entradvertissent de ne faire point de grandes enjambées, de peur de devenir garçons, comme Marie Germain. — I, 107.

He saith, that *upon a time* leaping, and straining himselfe *to overleape another, he wot not how, but where before he was a woman, he suddenly felt* the instrument of a man to come out of him; and to this day the maidens of *that towne and countrie* have a song in use, by which they warne one another, *when they are leaping, not to straine themselves overmuch*, or open their legs too wide, for feare they should bee turned to boies, as Marie Germane was. — I, 92.

Often, under the guise of dispensing information, Florio appears really to be stating his own views, or instructing the reader in what the cultivated man should think. Montaigne had written: "Ronsard & du Bellay," [1] but the translator wants to give them their proper estimation, and says "great Ronsarde and learned Bellay." [2] Florio shares the Elizabethan love of horses; he detests Catholics and poetasters; he approves of sport and disapproves of whores. And when a passage in Montaigne gives him an excuse for expressing an opinion or indulging his tastes, he is not slow to embrace it.

His interest in horses is quickly manifest in the essay "Of Steeds, called in French Destriers," when he twice enlarges the text. The extension of the statement, "Et un, qui seulement des dents, bridoit & harnachoit son

[1] I, 210.   [2] I, 182.

cheval"[1] into "And another, who only with teeth, *and without the helpe of any hand*, would bridle, *curry, rub, dresse, saddle, girt*, and harnish his horse,"[2] may be due in part to his simple delight in series of words. But in the other case the reason for the riot of language obviously lies in the translator's devotion to his subject:

Ce que j'ay admiré autresfois, de voir un cheval dressé à se manier à toutes mains, avec une baguette, la bride avallée sur ses oreilles. — I, 400.	That which I have other times wondered at, to see a horse fashioned *and taught*, that a man having but a wand in his hand, and his bridle loose hanging over his eares, might at his pleasure manage, *and make him turne, stop, run, cariere, trot, gallop, and whatever else may be expected of an excellent ready horse.* — I, 337.

More than once Florio's feeling is so ardent that he brings before us the whole pageant of an English hunt, especially when of "Cette secousse, & l'ardeur de ces huées, nous frappe"[3] he makes "That suddaine motion, *and riding*, and the earnestnesse of shouting, *jubeting, and hallowing, still* ringing *in our eares*."[4] In the essay where Montaigne showed that he did not share the cruelty of the Renaissance, and wrote "Je . . . ois impatiemment gemir un lievre sous les dents de mes chiens,"[5] Florio translates: "I cannot well endure a *seelie dew-bedabled* hare to groane when she is seized upon by the houndes."[6] Here his warmth of perception lent him a stroke of genius not unworthy of the greatest.

[1] I, 404.   [2] I, 341.   [3] II, 138.
[4] II, 120.   [5] II, 137.   [6] II, 119.

As a resolute Protestant, Florio feels it his duty where Montaigne had spoken of "les erreurs de Wiclef" [1] to change it to "Wickliff's opinions." [2] As a devotee of the Muses his furious rhetoric is taxed to the full to express his comtempt for poetasters: "Since *great* Ronsarde and *learned* Bellay have raised our French Poesie *unto that height of honour*, where it now is: I see not one of *these petty-ballad-makers, or* prentise-*dogrell* rymers, that doth not *bumbast his labours with high*-swelling *and heaven-disimbowelling* words." [3] Montaigne had written with reserve, "Depuis que Ronsard & du Bellay ont donné credit à nostre poësie Françoise, je ne vois si petit apprenti, qui n'enfle des mots." [4] No less contumely is heaped by Florio upon one whom Montaigne described as "l'autre vestue en garce, coiffée d'un attiffet emperlé." [5] Florio knows what he thinks about her sort, and says, "the other *disguised and* drest about the head like *unto an impudent* harlot, with *embroyderies, frizelings, and* carcanets of pearles." [6] On the other hand, the translator finds worthy not only the bearing of arms, but other exercises as well, and in his additions of "wrestling" and "riding of a horse," [7] Roger Ascham would have agreed with him. In the essay on the education of

[1] I, 18.   [2] I, 25.   [3] I, 182.
[4] I, 211.   [5] I, 198.   [6] I, 171.
[7] The two texts read: "Qui par souhait ne trouve plus plaisant & plus doux, revenir poudreux et victorieux d'un combat, que de la palme ou du bal," I, 199; "Who for pleasures sake doth not deeme it more delightsome to returne *all sweatie and* wearie from a victorious combat, *from wrestling, or riding of a horse*, than from a Tennis-court, or dancing schoole," I, 172.

children, Florio not only shows his interest in the subject, but also reminds us he is an Italian by inserting, in connection with the theme that philosophy can be wooed only by the noble, a long quotation, beginning "For, as famous Torquato Tasso saith." [1]

It has been stated that the language of Montaigne was sometimes too coarse for his translator,[2] who wished to tone his book to English ears. Occasionally we do find Florio speaking euphemistically; for example, when for the blunt "Ils en montrent d'autant plus de cul, qu'ils esperent en hausser la teste" [3] he substitutes "By how much more they hoped to raise their head, so much more do they show their simplicity." [4] But if this reticence is owing to modesty, it is a modesty which sometimes takes strange forms. Once, to be sure, he does indicate a rough word by a dash, but only because he has made the expression even stronger than the original.[5] At another he cuts short an offensive anecdote, but after he has already told half! It is narrated how "Aesope that famous man saw his Master pisse as he was walking: What (said hee) must we not etc. when we are running?" [6] Florio took liberties with his author, but that least excusable one of prudery cannot be charged against him.

---

[1] I, 153.   [2] Dieckow, p. 19.

[3] IV, 149.   [4] III, 279.

[5] "A —— in the fooles teeth," I, 252, for "bren du fat," I, 298.

[6] III, 392 ("Esope ce grand homme vid son maistre qui pissoit en se promenant, Quoy donq, fit-il, nous faudra-il chier en courant?" IV, 281).

V

Florio's greatest gift was the ability to make his book come to life for the Elizabethan imagination. Approximately the same forces surged through France and England in the Renaissance, but if Montaigne was to be fused into an integral part of the English mind and not left as a foreign classic, not only his spirit but the form of his expression had to be naturalized. And throughout his translation, sometimes consciously, more often instinctively, Florio creates a Montaigne who is an actual Elizabethan figure.

His speech assumes the high-flung pitch of his new surroundings. Florio was no poet, but he shared some of the qualities which make it so often appear that the Englishman of the late-sixteenth century wrote with greater ease in poetry than in prose. He speaks of the "heavens wide-bounding vault," [1] "swift-gliding Time," [2] the sun's "all-seeing eye," [3] and "many-headed confusion," [4] with absolutely no hint from Montaigne. "Sa pyramide" [5] is "his high-towring Pyramis, or Heaven-menacing Tower," [6] "de l'ombre et du doubte," [7] "from out the shadow of oblivion or dungeon of doubt." [8] Similar phrases characterize the great flow

[1] II, 251 ("la voute celeste," II, 288).
[2] II, 502 ("le temps," III, 196).
[3] I, 228 ("ses yeux," I, 267).
[4] III, 301 ("cette confusion," IV, 175).
[5] II, 310.   [6] II, 270.
[7] III, 353.   [8] III, 96.

of Elizabethan verse; and Florio's, to be sure, have no originality, but are repetitions of the accepted convention. In accordance, too, with the demands of this convention he introduces classic allusions. "Le soleil" [1] becomes "Phoebus" [2] bearing his "mourning weedes." "No human judgment is so vigilant or Argos-eied" [3] is his rendering of "Il n'est jugement humain si tendu." [4] Usually these poeticisms add little, but once at least we feel the alchemy of imagination, when "la verdeur des ans" [5] becomes "the Aprill of my yeares." [6]

The translator is constantly trying to discover a way to substitute the concrete for the abstract, to give color to an idea by an image. When Montaigne states an aphorism, "Mais aucun bien sans peine," [7] Florio pours new life into it: "But no good without paines; no Roses without prickles." [8] In addition to the general statement is an illustration; there is not only an appeal to the mind, but an appeal to the eye. "Men of their coate" [9] for "hommes de leur sorte" [10] achieves power of suggestion through being definite. In countless other cases the introduction of a graphic detail brings a new vividness and intimacy to the plain statement of the idea. Examples are everywhere: "to play the wilie Foxe" [11] for "de faire le fin," [12] "in the twinkling of an eye" [13] for "en un moment," [14] and the especially felicitious "to

---

[1] II, 386.   [2] II, 334.   [3] II, 258.   [4] II, 296.
[5] III, 318.   [6] III, 65.   [7] III, 298.   [8] III, 49.
[9] III, 236.   [10] IV, 99.   [11] II, 308.
[12] II, 354.   [13] III, 139. [14] III, 404.

goe about to catch the winde in a net" [1] for "de negocier au vent." [2] On the occasions where Montaigne himself had used an image, Florio develops it more fully with uncalled-for but charming detail. To the French proverb "Ce sont les pieds du paon, qui abbatent son orgueil," [3] Florio adds, "It is *the foulenesse of* the Peacockes feete, which doth abate his pride, *and stoope his gloating-eyed tayle*." [4] And when he translates "cercher le vent de la faveur des Roys" [5] into "to seeke after court holy-water and wavering-favours of Princes," [6] he uses a phrase that may have caught Shakespeare's eye, and have been appropriated for the Fool's speech in Lear: "O Nunkle, court holy-water in a dry house, is better than this rain-water, out o' doore." [7]

His frequent development of metaphors from sea terms gives a hint of how his book spoke the daily tongue of the nation whose life centered on its ships. He writes they "have no other anker" [8] for "qui n'ont appuy que," [9] and "Being once embarked, one must either go on or sinke" [10] for the less distinct "Depuis qu'on y est, il faut aller ou crever." [11] "Les orages et tempestes se piquent" [12] becomes more visual in "the

---

[1] I, 271. [2] I, 321. [3] III, 364.
[4] III, 105. [5] I, 344. [6] I, 289.

[7] *Lear*, III, ii. This phrase was not used by Shakespeare before the appearance of Florio's translation, so it is a reasonable assumption that it may first have fixed his attention in the *Essays*. However, it had appeared in the language earlier, the first reading in the *New English Dictionary* being 1583, Golding, *Calvin on Deuteronomy*; also 1598, in Florio's own *Worlde of Wordes*.

[8] I, 115. [9] I, 135. [10] III, 275.
[11] IV, 144. [12] I, 80.

sea-billowes and surging waves rage and storme." [1]
Twice Florio uses a variation of the popular saying "to
have an oar in every water": once when he substitutes
it for the French idiom "à mettre le nez par tout"; [2] and
again in the rendering, which deserves to be famous, of
"Aristote qui remue toutes choses" [3] by "Aristotle that
hath an oare in every water and medleth with all
things." [4]

The translator continually makes such alterations for
the sake of a fuller picture. Montaigne's statement that
the cannibals eat "sans autre artifice que de les cuire" [5]
is entirely adequate for anyone but Florio, who expands
it to "without any sauces, or skill of Cookerie, but plaine
boiled or broiled." [6] His most confirmed habit is to draw
fresh illustrations which have been suggested to him by
the text. The fact that these are never needed by no
means diminishes their richness. For instance, take the
passage where Montaigne is saying how little the world
loses by his essays:

Tout le commerce que j'ay en cecy avec le publicq, c'est que j'emprunte les utils de son escriture, plus soudaine & plus aisée. En recompense, j'empescheray peut estre, que quelque coin de beurre ne se fonde au marché. — III, 64.	All the commerce I have in this with the world is, that I borrow the instruments of their writing, as more speedy, and more easie: in requitall whereof I may peradventure hinder the melting of some piece of butter in the market, *or a Grocer from selling an ounce of pepper.* — II, 400.

---

[1] I, 69.　　[2] I, 226 (Florio, I, 196).　　[3] I, 16.
[4] I, 23.　　[5] I, 260.　　[6] I, 223.

The same tendency crops out in the facetious quip Florio tags to the end of a quotation from Livy: "Equi sine froenis, deformis ipse cursus, rigida cervice et extento capite currentium: 'the horses being without bridles, their course is ill-favoured, they running with a stiffe necke, and outstretch't head' (*like a roasted Pigge*)." [1]

The picture and action of a situation are always uppermost in his mind. It is an instinct of his nature to write "with a vaile over his face" [2] for "le visage couvert," [3] "the skittish and loose-broken jade" [4] for "le cheval eschappé," [4] or the striking "headlong tumbled downe from some rocke" [5] for "precipitez." [6] The desire for a feeling of motion is the force underlying nearly all his additions. He wants always to increase the emphasis, to heighten and magnify. Such striving for action reveals itself time and again in the use of a strong verb. "I flie a lower pitch," [7] he writes for "je suis d'un point plus bas"; [8] and "we have harped long enough upon one string" [9] for "en voyla assez." [10] In his compounds this sense of movement is even greater: "harme-working eyes," [11] and "certaine terror-moving engines," [12] for Montaigne's adjectives "nuisans," [13] and "espouventables." [14] Sometimes Florio achieves the emphasis he

[1] I, 338 (Montaigne, of course, did not translate the Latin, I, 400).
[2] I, 18.   [3] I, 10.   [4] I, 40.   [5] I, 67.
[6] I, 78.   [7] III, 227.   [8] IV, 88.
[9] II, 536.   [10] III, 237. [11] I, 100.
[12] I, 136.   [13] I, 116.   [14] I, 161.

wants by underlining the idea or by increasing its range. "Le Savoïard" [1] who can conceive of no greater man than his master becomes "that dull-pated Savoyard." [2] Frequently Florio records a shade of meaning which the nature of the situation has suggested to him. "Le païsant et le cordonnier" [3] are given characteristics: "the plaine husbandman or the unwilie shoomaker." [4] "Cette ridicule piece" [5] becomes "that laughter-moving and maids looke-drawing piece," [6] which provoked so many broad remarks on the London stage.

In practically every case, as has already been suggested, these alterations of Florio's are dictated by a theatrical sense. The habit of seeing and saying things dramatically is one of the most distinctive qualities in the Elizabethan temperament. The dramatic imagination is by essence concrete. Its appeal is to the eye, it must gain its effect through the portrayal of definite events. The dramatist's method, therefore, consists in taking a situation and heightening its pitch by a skillful exaggeration of tone and by a hint of action in the swing and cadence of his words. Such also is Florio's method, and it permeates his treatment of Montaigne. Shakespeare was not alone in conceiving all the world as a stage: it was the contemporary outlook on life. Montaigne, discussing how hard it was for a man to describe

[1] I, 192.   [2] I, 165.
[3] I, 167.   [4] I, 140.
[5] III, 339.   [6] III, 83.

his own nature, had remarked: "Encore se faut il tes-
tonner, encore se faut il ordonner & renger pour sortir
en place." [1] And Florio makes it: "Yet must a man
handsomely trimme-up, yea and dispose and range himselfe *to appeare on the Theatre of this world*." [2]

Florio's sense of the dramatic is the central force
molding his prose. It determines not only the manner in
which he builds upon Montaigne's situations, but also
his addition of words, not for their meaning, but for
their rhythm. When Florio heightens the content,
sometimes it is the splendor, sometimes the pathos, more
often the sheer excitement of the situation that catches
him. When Montaigne describes how dangerous it is
for a city which has come to terms with the enemy to
give "l'entree libre aux soldats," [3] it is part of the Elizabethan nature to call them "the needie, bloudthirstie
and prey-greedy" soldiers.[4] Florio plunges so deeply
into the spirit of a situation and feels it so poignantly
that it becomes his own, and he is no longer translating,
but envisaging the scene anew. In any situation it is
the elements of contrast that focus his attention, and he
develops them with the instinct of the dramatist, doing
everything he can to heighten the effect. Examples are
so common that they can be chosen almost at random.
Sometimes, however, Florio outdoes himself. Then the
scene absorbs him so completely that he is practically

[1] II, 64.   [2] II, 59.
[3] I, 32.   [4] I, 35.

writing a new book. For instance, in the essay "Of Physiognomy," where Montaigne gave an account of how, although unarmed, his resolute appearance once caused an enemy captain to withdraw from his hall, Florio's imagination dramatizes the picture far more fully:

Il remonte à cheval, ses gens ayants continuellement les yeux sur luy, pour voir quel signe il leur donneroit: bien estonnez de le voir sortir et abandonner son advantage. — IV, 203.

What shall I say more? He *bids me farewell, calleth for* his horse, gets up, *and offreth to be gone,* his people having continually their eyes *fixed* upon him, to *observe his lookes,* and see what signe he should make unto them: much amazed to see him be gone, *and wondring to see him omit* and forsake such an advantage. — III, 325.

And perhaps the most astonishing example of all, where words run riot, and yet Florio succeeds in maintaining strength of unity and adding a fullness and color:

L'avaricieux le prie pour la conservation vaine & superflue de ses thresors: l'ambitieux pour ses victoires, & conduite de sa fortune: le voleur l'employe à son ayde, pour franchir le hazard & les difficultez, qui s'opposent à l'execution de ses meschantes entreprinses: ou le remercie de l'aisance qu'il a trouvé à desgosiller un passant. Au pied de la maison, qu'ils vont escheller ou petarder, ils font leurs prieres, l'intention et l'esperance pleine

The covetous man *sueth and* praieth unto him for the vaine *increase* and superfluous preservation of his *wrong-gotten* treasure. The ambitious, *he importuneth God* for the conduct of his fortune, *and that he may have* the victorie *of all his desseignes.* The theefe, *the pirate, the murtherer, yea and the traitor, all call upon him, all implore* his aid, *and all solicite him, to give them courage in their attempts, constancie in their resolutions,* to remove all

de cruauté, de luxure, & d'ava-
rice. — I, 443.

lets and difficulties, that *in any
sort* may withstand their wicked
executions, *and impious* actions;
or give him thanks,[1] *if they have
had good successe; the one if he
have met with a good bootie, the
other if he returne home rich, the
third if no man have seen him kill
his enemie, and the last, though
he have caused any execrable mis-
chiefe.*[1] *The Souldier,* if he but
goe *to besiege a cottage,* to scale *a
Castle, to rob a Church,* to pettard
a gate, to force a *religious* house,
*or any villanous act, before he at-
tempt it,* praieth *to God for his assistance,* though his intents and
hopes be full-*fraught* with
crueltie, *murther,* covetise, lux-
urie, *sacrilege and all iniquitie.* —
I, 373-374.

In none of these instances do Florio's additions clog
the movement of his prose. He possesses a strong sense
of rhythm, and frequently introduces words purely for
the sake of it. Many of his doublets are put in for the
beat of the language: "For, as in matters of husbandrie,
the labor that must be used before *sowing, setting,* and
planting, yea in planting itselfe, is most certaine and
easie. But when that which was *sowen, set* and planted,
commeth to take life. . . ." [2] Here, as often, compactness of sense has been sacrificed to the feeling for words.

[1] All this for "de l'aisance qu'il a trouvé à degosiller un passant!"

[2] I, 152 ("Tout ainsi qu'en l'agriculture, les façons, qui vont devant le
planter, sont certaines & aysées, & le planter mesme. Mais depuis que ce qui
est planté, vient à prendre vie. . . ." I, 180).

Florio, caught by a rhythm, develops it with a rhetorical swing foreign to Montaigne. Often he attains a rich fullness, sometimes — as in this passage on the fear of death — a movement of force and solemnity: "But *when* that last part of death, and of our selves *comes to be acted*, then no dissembling will availe, then it is high time to speake plaine English, *and put off all vizards*: then whatsoever the pot containeth must be shewne, be it good *or bad*, *foule or* cleane, *wine or water*." [1]

Too often, however, as we have seen, he is led into heaping up words until they clutter the sentence and plunge it into obscure fustian. Such unhappy additions are of the type that make him write "his succeeding posteritie," [2] "bounteous liberality," [3] and "free liberty," [4] and give to many passages the feeling of being swollen and over-ripe. Florio is unable to curb his habit of doubling, even in sentences already extended. The result is that Montaigne's balance and rhythm are destroyed, and the force and crispness of his style disintegrate. Florio is not often able to perceive the strength of simplicity, and this limitation leads him on occasions into his greatest fault, the loss of emotional power. In the essay, "Que Philosopher, c'est apprendre à mourir," Montaigne cites instances of those who have died young:

[1] I, 70 ("Mais à ce dernier rolle de la mort & de nous, il n'y a plus que faindre, il faut parler François; il faut montrer ce qu'il y a de bon et de net dans le fond du pot," I, 81).

[2] I, 61 ("sa posterité," I, 68).

[3] III, 143 ("liberalité," III, 408).

[4] *Ibid.* ("franchise").

"Il est plein de raison, & de pieté, de prendre exemple de l'humanité mesme de Jesus-Christ. Or il finit sa vie à trente & trois ans. Le plus grand homme, simplement homme, Alexandre, mourut aussi à ce terme." [1] The affecting directness of this is ignored by Florio, who expands the last sentence into the trivial: "The greatest man that ever was being no more than a man, I meane Alexander the great, ended his dayes, and died also of that age." [2]

Yet everything that Florio does to Montaigne is calculated to bring the *Essays* closer to the spirit of his time. Words and expressions of Elizabethan flavor crowd every page: "mumpes and mowes," [3] "blockish asses," [4] "meere bug-beares and scar-crowes, to scare birdes with all" [5] appear in place of Montaigne's plain "grimaces," [6] "des asniers," [7] "vrais epouvantails de cheneviere." [8] "I doe beware and keepe myselfe from such treasons, and cunny-catching in mine owne bosome" [9] is the wholly characteristic version of "Je me sauve de telles trahisons en mon propre giron." [10] Nouns are used for verbs or adjectives: "in a strange and foe country" [11] for "en terre ennemie." [12] Constant alterations are made in Montaigne's phrasing to introduce native idioms. "Respondirent à sa barbe" [13] is shifted to "answered him to his teeth"; [14] "sans suitte" [15] is given

[1] I, 88.	[2] I, 75.	[3] III, 60.	[4] I, 136.
[5] II, 76.	[6] III, 312.	[7] I, 162.	[8] II, 86.
[9] II, 79.	[10] II, 89.	[11] I, 129.	[12] I, 153.
[13] I, 16.	[14] I, 23.	[15] I, 167.	

the fullness of "without rime or reason, sans head or foot." [1] Even more striking is the colloquial tone that Florio adopts. "God wot," "Well," "Marry, what you list" come frequently, and never with any counterpart in the original. "'Tut-tut,' said he, 'it is alreadie finished'" [2] for the simple "Elle est composée & preste" [3] reveals at a glance the greatness of this change. To the same purpose is the translator's varied use of rich proverbial phrases where none had appeared in the French: "to set the foolish and the wise, us and beasts all in one ranke: *no barrell better Hering*." [4]

In all these ways Florio gives the *Essays* intimacy and warmth. He makes sure that the book will not remain in the study but will be read by everyone. He can write colloquial English at its best: "If I chance to call one knave or asse, my purpose is not for ever to enfeoffe him with those nick-names; nor do I thinke to say, tong thou liest, if immediately after I call him an honest man." [5] And he sometimes produces a sturdiness that suggests the temper of the Elizabethan seamen: "We see our *carowsing tospot* German souldiers, when they are most plunged in their cups, *and as drunke as Rats*, to have per-

[1] I, 141.

[2] I, 182.

[3] I, 210.

[4] III, 105 ("apparier les fols et les sages, et nous et les bestes," III, 364).

[5] I, 252 ("Quand je l'appelle un badin, un veau: je n'entrepren pas de luy coudre à jamais ces titres: ny ne pense me desdire, pour le nommer honeste homme tantost après," I, 298).

fect remembrance of their quarter, of the watch word, and of their files." [1]

Whenever necessary Florio works slight changes to bring the book home to his audience. "Une harangere de Petit pont" [2] becomes her familiar London counterpart "any Oyster-wife about the streets." [3] In the essay "Of Names," when Montaigne wanted to illustrate how the Emperor Geta would have served at his table only those dishes beginning with the same letter, he cited those "qui se commençoient par m: mouton, marcassin, merlus, marsoin." [4] Florio finds he can do better with "those that began with P: as pig, pie, pike, puddings, pouts, porke, pancakes," [5] and inevitably doubles the list. It is the same with: "Every several nation hath some names, which, I wot not how, are sometimes taken in ill part, as with us Jacke, Hodge, Tom, Will, Bat, Benet, and so forth." [6] Montaigne had used "Jehan, Guillaume, Benoist." [7] "A Ploughman" [8] is substituted for "un vigneron," [9] that is, an English occupation for a French one. The apparitions that appear to poor people are not "des Loups-garoups, des Lutins, & des Chimeres," [10] but "Larves, Hobgoblins, Robbin-good-fellowes, and such other Bug-beares and Chimeraes." [11] "Tel allegue Platon & Homer, qui ne les vid onques" [12]

[1] II, 15 ("Nous voyons nos Allemans noyez dans le vin, se souvenir de leur quartier, du mot, et de leur rang," II, 13).

[2] I, 209.   [3] I, 180.   [4] I, 379.   [5] I, 318.
[6] I, 317.   [7] I, 378.   [8] III, 196.   [9] IV, 54.
[10] I, 75.   [11] I, 65.   [12] IV, 195.

is expanded to "Some alleadge Plato, some mention Homer, that never saw them, or as they say in English, 'Many a man speakes of Robinhood, that never shot in his bow.'" [1]

Native customs and usages, and a strong national feeling, color every line. Montaigne declared that it was no wonder we could not understand the animals since "aussi ne faisons nous les Basques et les Troglodytes"; [2] Florio makes it "no more do we the Cornish, the Welch, or Irish." [3] When a fond father wanted to rise out of his class and make his son "maistre Jean, ou maistre Pierre ... un beau notaire de village," [4] the English translator is more outspoken in his ridicule of "Sir John Lackelatine, or Master Peter an Oake ... a country Notary, or Petty-fogging Clark." [5] Whenever possible Florio adds a significant English phrase to a series to extend the reader's range of idea: "so many innovations of estates, *so many fals of Princes*, and changes of publike fortune"[6] for "tant de remuements d'estat, & changements de fortune publique." [7] Montaigne discussed the bad practice of putting into children's hands "des Lancelots du Lac, des Amadis, des Huons de Bordeaux, & tels fatras de livres." [8] To these Florio joins "King Arthur," and characterizes them all as "such idle time consuming and wit-besotting trash of bookes," [9] with which severe dis-

---

[1] III, 318. [2] II, 168. [3] II, 145.
[4] III, 227. [5] II, 528. [6] I, 166.
[7] I, 193. [8] I, 217. [9] I, 188.

approval of popular reading the followers of Ascham would have concurred.

Whether by the suggestion in his speech of English countrysides and ports, or by his enthusiasm for the contemporary London literary vogues, or by his constant hint of native opinions and habits and ways of thought, Florio created an Elizabethan book. Not the least attraction for his contemporaries were the quotations from the classics and French and Italian, the translations of which were probably for the most part the work of Dr. Gwinne.[1] As poetry these are curious. They frequently have vigor:

> Fear then unbreasts all wit
> That in my mind doth sit.

"Unbreasts," as Mr. Saintsbury has remarked, for a literal rendering of the verb in Ennius' "Tum pavor sapientiam omnem mihi ex animo expectorat" is as happy as it is daring. Again, when the translation happens to be from Horace, there is a crisp and suitable sententiousness:

> Set times and moods, make you the first word last,
> The last word first, as if they were new cast:
> Yet find th' unjoynted Poets joints stand fast.

[1] Florio states in his preface: "So Scholler-like did he [i. e., Maister Doctor Guinne] undertake what Latine prose; Greeke, Latine, Italian or French Poesie should crosse my way (which as Bugge-beares affrighted my unacquaintance with them)." This might simply mean that Gwinne had traced the quotations to their sources. But the fact that he wrote copious prefatory verses (under the title "Il Candido") for both the *Worlde of Wordes* and the *Essays* would indicate him as the poet here.

On the other hand, Florio's introduction of rhymes and his almost invariable habit of turning a single line into a couplet have the disturbing effect of making Vergil, Seneca, Ovid, Du Bellay, and Tasso all sound exactly the same. It may be no grave objection that the sense is sometimes altered to suit the rhyme,[1] but it is grave indeed when so many rich cadences are turned into the jingle of the mottoes we are now accustomed to find with the paper cap in a birthday-party snapper:

> Be thou when with thee is not any
> As good unto thy selfe as many.[2]

VI

Such blemishes do not seem to have disturbed the Elizabethans. Florio's book enjoyed great popularity, and a second handsome edition appeared in 1613. By this time the translator had long held the appointments of gentleman-extraordinary and groom of the privy chamber, and reader in Italian to the Queen, at the

---

[1] For example,

> "Yeares had I (to make even)
> Scarse two above eleven"

for

> "Alter ab undecimo tum me vix ceperat annus." (Virgil.)

Occasionally the translator also runs the poet's name into the verse:

> "Endevour they things to them to submit,
> Not them to things (if they have Horace wit)"

for

> "Conentur sibi res, non se submittere rebus."

[2] "In solis sis tibi turba locis." (Tibullus.)

salary of £100 a year. He was a person of consequence, who was soon to receive from the College of Heralds the right to the arms of a gentleman.[1] He had been married, probably to Rose Daniel,[2] sister of the poet, and had a daughter Aurelia. In the year of the first appearance of his *Montaigne*, Nicholas Breton had dedicated to him *A Mad World, My Masters*, and in 1610 John Healey had chosen him as the patron for a translation of Epictetus. So when he published his enlarged *New World of Words* in 1611 and two years later brought out another edition of the *Essays*, he could be satisfied with dedicating his work to no one but Queen Anne herself. The cavalier tone of the now brief notice to the reader is amusing:

Enough, if not too much, hath beene said of this Translation. If the faults found even by my selfe in the first impression, be now by the Printer corrected, as he was directed, the worke is much amended: If not, know that through mine attendance on her Majesty, I could not intend it; and blame not Neptune for thy second shipwracke.

The faults had not been corrected; indeed they were far more numerous than in the first impression. But "still resolute" John Florio's thoughts had been so constantly on the court and Her Majesty's Italian lessons during these ten years that such trifles were beneath his notice.

---

[1] "A marigold proper issuing from the stalk, sprouting out of two leaves. In chief the sun in splendour proper."

[2] In the first edition of the *Essays*, Daniel addressed his prefatory verses "To my deere friend M. John Florio"; in the second edition, this had been changed to "To my deere brother and friend." Wood states that Queen Anne was a favorer of Daniel's muse, "as she was of Jo. Florio, who married Sam. Daniel's sister." *Athenae Oxonienses*, ed. P. Bliss (London, 1815), II, 269.

Florio continued to thrive at court until the queen's death in 1618. Then he retired with his second wife to the place he had bought at Fulham, lived in obscurity and apparent poverty, and died a victim of the plague in 1626. In his will he regrets that he cannot leave more to his "beloved consort and painful nurse," and commits her to the protection of the Earl of Pembroke. To him he bequeaths all his "Italian, French and Spanish bookes, as well printed as unprinted, being in number about Three hundred and Fortie," his "new perfect Dictionary," and

the Corund stone (as a jewell fitt for a Prince) W^ch Ferdinando the great Duke of Tuscanie sent as a most precious gift (among divers others) unto Queene Anne of blessed memory, the use and vertue whereof is written in twoe peeces of paper both in Italian and English being in a little box with the stone.[1]

Florio's success had not been confined to the court. His *Montaigne* had reached the mind and emotions of England. Ben Jonson suggests its vogue, when, in the third act of *Volpone* (1605), he makes Lady Politick Would-be say, in speaking of Guarini's *Pastor Fido*:

> All our English writers,
> I mean such as are happy in the Italian,
> Will deign to steal out of this author, mainly;
> Almost as much as from Montaignie.

Jonson himself had not been insensible to the influence. He might later write in his *Discoveries* slurring remarks

[1] This will was printed by Chambrun, pp. 219-221.

about the scattered quality of all essayists, "even their master Montaigne";[1] but the British Museum possesses a copy of Florio's 1603 edition with what is regarded as an authentic Jonson autograph, and also a presentation copy of *Volpone* with the following inscription: "To his loving Father, & worthy Freinde, Mr. John Florio, the ayde of his Muses, Ben Jonson seales this testimony of Freindeship & Love." And that Jonson had felt the attraction of his friend's translation[2] is revealed in the very manner of the casual thoughts and reflections in his *Discoveries*. The two men discuss a very great number of the same topics; but it is obvious, as in the case of Bacon and Montaigne, that both could have drawn them from their reading or the store of their experience. However, the coincidence becomes more striking when we find them both telling the same anecdotes, both reflecting that undue eagerness only hinders us, and agreeing that old age is a disease; and when Montaigne describes the mind and Jonson the soul as entangling herself in her wanderings like a silkworm,[3] it

---

[1] Jonson, *Works*, IX, 158.

[2] Of course Jonson might also have read the original, but in this regard it is well to remember Drummond's remark: "He neither doth understand French nor Italiannes." "Conversations with Drummond," *Works*, IX, 371.

[3] Montaigne: "Il [l'esprit] ne faict que fureter & quester; & va sans cesse, tournoyant, bastissant, & s'empestrant, en sa besongne: comme nos vers à soye, & s'y estouffe," IV, 212.

Florio: "[The minde] doth but quest and ferret, and uncessantly goeth turning, winding, building and entangling hirselfe in her owne worke; as doe our silke-wormes, and therein stifleth hir selfe," III, 331–332.

Jonson: "[The soul] is a perpetual agent, prompt and subtle; but often flexible, and erring, intangling herself like a silk-worm," IX, 161.

becomes impossible not to conclude that Jonson's mind had been frequently absorbed in the *Essays*.

Other Jacobean figures had also felt their power. The one English work produced wholly in the spirit of Montaigne is Sir Walter Raleigh's essay "The Skeptick," written during his imprisonment in the Tower. Raleigh's theme is that "the Skeptick doth neither affirm, neither deny any Position; but doubteth of it, and opposeth his Reasons against that which is affirmed, or denied, to justify his not consenting." [1] He then argues against the certainty of knowledge, chiefly on two grounds: that the variability of our sense impressions makes them unreliable; and that man's belief in his great mental superiority over beasts is unfounded. On both these topics the parallels with Montaigne's "Apology for Raymond Sebond" are very close.[2] Drummond wrote a "Song" in the spirit of the essay "Que Philosopher, c'est apprendre à mourir." Burton cited the Frenchman time and again, always with the tone of a disciple, and devoted one of the sections in *The Anatomy of Melancholy* to the "Force of Imagination," the same theme that Montaigne had treated in one of his essays. Both Drummond and Burton, as well as Raleigh, may well have drawn their chief stimulus directly from the French. But this is not true of Shakespeare.

Shakespeare's reaction to Florio's translation reveals

---

[1] Raleigh, *Works*, ed. Birch (London, 1751), II, 331.
[2] See Upham, pp. 540–544.

in epitome the reaction of his age. He read the book fervently, for he found in it much that appealed to the temper of his own thought. He caught words and phrases from it instinctively, rhetorical turns of speech, suggestions for images and for ideas. It fired his mind, and gave a charged expression to much that had previously been unformulated and latent. In short, to use the effective comparison of the latest writer on this subject, Shakespeare was affected by Montaigne in much the same manner as modern readers are by Shakespeare.[1] It would be dangerous to press too far the striking similarities in speech and thought,[2] since these might well spring "from the natural kinship of questioning minds." [3] Most general ideas are the common property of an age. Shakespeare and Montaigne both read Plutarch. Shakespeare and Florio were constantly talking with the same people, hearing the same theories, breathing the same air.[4]

[1] This stimulating idea is formulated by G. C. Taylor, *Shakspere's Debt to Montaigne* (Harvard University Press, 1925), p. 41. Mr. Taylor's book is an excellent summary of the whole question, and much that I say is a mere digest of his material.

[2] Needless to say they have been pressed too far in such a work as G. F. Stedefeld, *Hamlet: ein Tendenzdrama Shakespeare's gegen die skeptische und kosmopolitische Weltanschauung des Michael de Montaigne* (Berlin, 1871). Jacob Feis, *Shakspere and Montaigne* (London, 1884) develops the thesis that Shakespeare wrote Hamlet to discredit Montaigne's dangerous philosophy.

[3] W. Raleigh, *Shakespeare* (London, 1907), p. 76.

[4] From the undoubted acquaintance of Shakespeare and Florio, Chambrun (among others) has developed (pp. 100 ff.) an elaborate, entertaining, and far-fetched theory of a literary jealousy that found its expression in Shakespeare's representation of Florio as Holofernes in *Love's Labour's Lost*.

But, on the other hand, not only does Gonzalo's conception of the ideal commonwealth in the second act of *The Tempest* coincide almost exactly with a passage in the essay "Of the Caniballes"; [1] but in *Lear* and in the other plays immediately following the appearance of Florio's translation, when Shakespeare's characters utter the burden of their thoughts, they echo again and again the words of Montaigne.[2] When Hamlet says,

> There's a divinity that shapes our ends
> Rough-hew them how we will,

there is an undoubted coincidence in thought and expression with Montaigne's statement: "My consultation

---

[1] Florio: "It is a nation, would I answer Plato, that hath *no kinde of traffike, no knowledge of Letters*, no intelligence of numbers, *no name of magistrate*, nor of politike superioritie; *no use of service, of riches or of povertie; no contracts*, no *successions*, no partitions, *no occupation but idle;* no respect of kindred, but common, no apparell but naturall, no manuring of lands, *no use of wine, corne, or mettle.*" I, 222.

Shakespeare:

> "I' the commonwealth I would by contraries
> Execute all things; for *no kind of traffic*
> Would I admit; *no name of magistrate;*
> *Letters should not be known; riches, poverty,*
> *And use of service, none; contract, succession,*
> Bourn, bound of land, tilth, vineyard, none;
> *No use of metal, corn, or wine,* or oil;
> *No occupation,* all men *idle,* all;
> And women too, but innocent and pure;
> No sovereignty; —" II, i.

How closely Shakespeare followed Florio is clear from the line, "No occupation, all men idle, all," which is a natural misunderstanding of the translator's rendering, "no occupation but idle," for Montaigne's "nulles occupations, qu'oysives."

[2] For a long list of parallel passages, including those that I cite here, see J. M. Robertson, *Montaigne and Shakespeare* (London, 1909).

doth somewhat roughly hew the matter, and by its first shew lightly consider the same: the main and chief point of the work I am wont to resign to Heaven." [1] The essay entitled "That the taste of Goods or Evils doth greatly depend on the opinion we have of them" [2] seems often the text for such lines as Iago's "'Tis in ourselves that we are thus or thus," or Hamlet's "There is nothing either good or bad but thinking makes it so." Similar ideas appear in both authors on the force of custom, on uncertainty and unhappiness, on death [3] and its likeness to sleep, on the divinity that doth hedge a king, on the splendor of the universe and the littleness of man. [4] Many of these, to be sure, are classic commonplaces, but it is significant that they do not appear to have been felt by Shakespeare until after he had read Florio. A great deal of ink has been spent in trying to account for the change in spirit that came over Shakespeare about the

[1] "Of the Art of Conferring," Book III, Essay 8.

[2] Book I, Essay 40.

[3] Florio: "The end of our cariere is death; it is the necessarie object of our aime; if it affright us, how is it possible we should step one foot further without an ague? . . . To what end recoile you from it, if you cannot goe backe?" Book I, Essay 19.

Shakespeare:

"Merely thou art death's fool;

For him thou labor'st by thy flight to shun,

And yet runns't toward him still." *Measure for Measure*, III, i.

[4] Florio: "the gods play at hand-ball with us and tosse us up and down on their handes." "Of Vanity," Book III, Essay 9.

Shakespeare:

"As flies to wanton boys, are we to the gods;

They kill us for their sport." *Lear* IV, i.

time of the accession of the new king. But it does not seem rash to assert that at least part of the representation in *Lear* of the vast and terrible forces of nature at play beyond the control of puny man, as well as part of the constant reiteration in all the plays after this time that "the strain of man's bred out into baboon and monkey," was due to the poet's violent reaction to some of the more somber elements in Montaigne. For the assumption that Florio's book had been a stirring experience is not based on the number of similar passages, but on more telling evidence. In *Shakspere's Debt to Montaigne*, Mr. Taylor has listed [1] seven hundred and fifty words and phrases from the plays which were not used by Shakespeare before 1603, and all of which appear in Florio. Sometimes indeed it was Florio who brought them into the language for the first time. Some of them are used by Shakespeare very often. They include many of the striking turns of speech that seem most characteristic of him: "caste the gorge at," "ever harping upon," [2] "in hugger-mugger," "mumps and mowes," [3] "nipping air," "set at naught," "take arms against," "tosse and turne," "things to come." Mr. Taylor's study has revealed that Shakespeare was affected by his reading of Florio in the way a man always is by a book which impresses him so deeply that it becomes an integral part of his life. Its form of expression frequently

---

[1] pp. 49–51, 58–66.
[2] Shakespeare: "still harping on."
[3] Shakespeare: "mops and mowes."

clung to him in the rhetorical shape of passages even where there is not the least connection with Montaigne's thought.[1] Shakespeare used these new words and phrases very often immediately after 1603, and then there is a gradual tapering off until *The Tempest*, where they again increase. This fact suggests an eager first reading that caused many phrases to stay half consciously in Shakespeare's memory for a period of years, and then a later return to the book which resulted in the passage on the ideal commonwealth.

VII

The English interest in Montaigne persisted so strongly that in 1685 Charles Cotton felt it the occasion for a new translation. His work reflects the change that was passing over English prose. It is clear, polished, and direct, but lacking in richness. The claim of his preface is that his errors are less gross and numerous than Florio's, and although he does smooth out many of the Elizabethan's confused heaps of words, he is himself guilty of a good many inaccuracies and several omissions. Under his hands extravagance and gusto are replaced by sharp crispness. The words are no longer felt as well as thought; and as a result one of the greatest

---

[1] Florio: "*Whereto serves* this mayden-like bashfulnesse ... *but to* increase a desire," Book II, Essay 15.
 Shakespeare:
> "*Whereto serves* mercy
> *But to* confront the visage of offence?" — *Hamlet*, III, iii.

charms is lost — the close intimacy of Florio's tone. So indefinable a quality is difficult to illustrate; but to one familiar with the spirit of the original it appears in a hundred small instances, such as Cotton's substitution in the opening words of the fourth essay of "A gentleman of my country" for "A gentleman of ours." [1] Cotton's cool formality becomes perhaps more apparent in the passages where the emotion is highly charged. In one of the many places where Montaigne speaks of the memory of his dead friend Etienne de la Boetie, Florio translates:

> There is no comfort so sweet in the losse of friends, as that our owne knowledge or conscience tels us, we never omitted to tell them everything, and expostulate all matters unto them, and to have had a perfect and free communication with them. Tell me my good friend, am I the better or the worse by having a taste of it? Surely I am much the better.[2]

With Cotton it becomes:

> There is not so sweet a Consolation in the loss of Friends, as the Consciousness of having had no Reserve or Secret for them; and to have had with them a perfect and entire Communication. Oh my Friend! am I the better for being sensible of this; or am I the worse? I am doubtless much the better.[3]

The fullness of Florio's rhythm has disappeared; the poignancy of his closing sentences has been turned into trimness and propriety.

[1] Montaigne: "Un Gentil-homme des nostres."   [2] II, 80.
[3] *Montaigne's Essays*, translated by Charles Cotton, 6th ed. (London, 1743), II, 73.

Cotton's translation passed through a long series of editions, and seems to have held the field until near the close of the last century when Florio once more came into his own.[1] Within the last three years, after a lapse of more than two hundred and forty since Cotton's effort, two new translations have been made, one in America by Mr. G. B. Ives,[2] and one in England by Mr. E. J. Trechmann.[3] With the exception of the former's absurdity in leaving untranslated every sentence which mentions sex (the only beneficial result of which will be an incentive to young readers to study French), both achievements are in accordance with the best principles of scientific scholarship. Their prose is dignified and colloquial, and nothing intrudes between the reader and the author — none of Florio's affectation or quaint experiments. Mr. Trechmann in particular renders Montaigne very closely, often vividly: he gives the meaning more clearly than it has ever been given, and yet the lack of one quality makes this lucidity somewhat color-

[1] Notably in the edition by Henry Morley (1886), the Tudor Translation reprint (1892–93), and the edition by A. R. Waller (1897–98).

[2] *The Essays of Montaigne*, translated by G. B. Ives, with introductions by Grace Norton (Harvard University Press, 1925).

[3] *The Essays of Montaigne*, translated by E. J. Trechmann, with an introduction by J. M. Robertson (Oxford University Press, 1927). How much Montaigne has to say to the modern spirit is emphasized by the fact that still a third translation is now in progress by Mr. Jacob Zeitlin of the University of Illinois. This will be based on the Cotton text, and its extensive commentary will fill a very real need.

less. His version is an accurate reproduction, but it was impossible that Florio's peculiarly vital pulse should stir in its pages. For Florio wrote in an age that was being shaped by the same spirit that had given life to the book.

CHAPTER V

Philemon Holland
The Translator General

I

PHILEMON HOLLAND became a legend. Popular imagination transformed his pen into a magic instrument. His son Henry informed the world that his father had translated the whole of Plutarch's *Morals* with a single quill, so very remarkable a feat that Henry wrote these verses about it:

> This Booke I wrote with *one* poore Pen,
> Made of a grey Goose quill,
> A Pen I found it, us'd before,
> A Pen I leave it still.

This rare trophy — the legend continues — "was afterwards begged by an ancient gentlewoman (mother to a noble countess), who garnished it in silver, and kept it as a monument." [1] But there are other versions. The theme was marvelous for all the books of anecdote. Aubrey declares it to have been the *Livy* which was so translated, and implies that Lady Harington embel-

[1] *Reliquiae Hearnianae*, ed. P. Bliss (London, 1857), II, 525.

lished the pen, and enshrined it among her trophies.[1]
Fuller, in his description of Holland as one of the
Worthies of England, magnanimously extends the legend
to include "many of his works," and goes on to say that
the translator "solemnly kept" his pen, "and shewed
[it] to my reverend tutor Doctor Samuel Ward. It seems
he leaned very lightly on the nib thereof, though
weightily enough in another sense, performing not
slightly but solidly what he undertook."[2] Fuller also hit
upon the happy sobriquet of "the translator general in
his age," and said, "Those books alone of his turning
into English will make a country gentleman a competent
library for historians." The antiquary here expressed
the general opinion of Holland's contemporaries: in a
period of great translations he stood preëminent, the
very symbol for a translator, as Sidney was the symbol
for a gentleman. In fact, he was so preëminent that
when opinion had changed in the next age the Gothic
library shelves of the hero of *The Dunciad* were made to
groan beneath the weight of his volumes.[3]

[1] J. Aubrey, *Brief Lives*, ed. A. Clark (Oxford, 1898), I, 406.
[2] T. Fuller, *History of the Worthies of England*, ed. P. A. Nuttall (London, 1840), III, 287.
[3] "But, high above, more solid learning shone,
   The classics of an age that heard of none;
   There Caxton slept, with Wynkyn at his side,
   One clasped in wood, and one in strong cow-hide;
   There, sav'd by spice, like mummies, many a year,
   Dry bodies of divinity appear:
   De Lyra there a dreadful front extends,
   And here the groaning shelves Philemon bends."
                    Pope, *The Dunciad*, I, 147-154.

But Holland was secure from Pope's sneers. The days of his glory spanned the whole English Renaissance. He was born in 1552, in the same year as Spenser. He lingered on, active to the end, until 1637, the year of Ben Jonson's death. His dedications included three sovereigns, Elizabeth, James, and Charles. Unlike North, he was a complete scholar: he needed no intermediary French version, but went straight to the Greek and Latin, compared the original with the French and Italian translations, and used the work of all the learned commentators. His achievement was to bring half a dozen of the ripe works of classical antiquity into the full tide of English literature.

The most important events of his life took place in his study. The son of a Protestant minister who had been forced during Mary's reign to flee to the Continent with Miles Coverdale, Holland was educated at Chelmsford Grammar School and Cambridge. At Trinity he studied under Whitgift (who was later the Archbishop of Canterbury), took his M. A. and became a fellow. He soon turned to medicine, graduated with his doctor's degree, and by 1595 had settled at Coventry, where he was to pass the long remainder of his life. His medical practice seems to have been small; at least it gave him time for his folios. But his income was also small, and as he had married in 1579 and had "a great charge of children" (seven sons and three daughters), in the year 1608, already famous for his translations, he accepted the humble position of usher at the Coventry Free School. He remained at this task for twenty years, and when promotion to the headmastership finally came, he was seventy-six, too old for the burdens of the office, and so he resigned at the end of ten months. He was then without resources. All except one of his sons had already died. Near the end, his poverty was relieved by a small sum from the vice-chancellor of Cambridge, who made this note: "He translated diverse books, and for 60 years kept good hospitality, *Sit tota Coventria testis.*" [1]

He had not been without honor. Coventry was proud of him, and in 1612 its council bestowed upon him the freedom of the city. Five years later when James I passed through Warwickshire on his return from Scotland, Holland, who had already dedicated Plutarch's *Morals* to His Majesty, was the inevitable choice of the loyal citizens to receive the king with "a learned, elegant, and religious speech." [2] He did so with fitting pompousness, for which, say the *Annals*, "he was much praised." They also record that the translator "was in a suite of black satten" which had cost the city the handsome figure of £11 1s. 11d. Holland was grateful for its interest and had inscribed his *Ammianus Marcellinus* to "his Right Worshipfull, the Mayor, and his Brethren, the Aldermen of the Citie of Coventrie," declaring:

---

[1] T. Sharp, *Illustrative Papers on the History and Antiquities of the City of Coventry*, ed. W. G. Fretton (Birmingham, 1871), p. 182. The few pages devoted to Holland in this book give the fullest account of him that has yet been made.

[2] This was printed in 1622.

These Endeavours of mine whatsoever I dedicate unto your Worships, the chiefe Magistrate and grave Senate of this Citie; and that for divers respects: First, your wise and moderate government of the place, wherein I have so many yeares conversed, hath afforded unto me both quiet repose and meanes also to follow my studies: Secondly, the affectionate love that yee have alwaies borne to good literature, testified by courteous entertainment of learned men; by competent salaries allowed from time to time to such professors, as have peaceably and with discreet carriage bestowed their talents among you; by exhibition given to poore schollers in the Universitie; by erecting also of late, and maintaining of a faire Librarie, not exampled (without offense to others be it spoken) in many cities of the Realme.[1]

Anecdote adds to his portrait a few more ineffaceable strokes. A manuscript in his hand of Euclid's *Harmonics*, which was long preserved in the Free School library, was of such a distinguished Greek character that Baskerville is said to have formed his Greek font partly upon it. Philemon Angel, the translator's great-grandson and godson, gave to Anthony à Wood some rare details:

His intellectuals and his senses remained perfect until the eighty-fourth year of his age; and more especially his sight so good, that he never used spectacles in all his life; he was always of a spare and temperate diet, and seldom drank between meals. And was always of a peaceable and quiet spirit,

[1] Dedication to *The Romane Historie*, Containing such Acts and occurrents as passed under Constantius, Julianus, Jovianus, Valentinianus, and Valens, Emperoures. Digested into 18 Bookes, the remains of 31 and written first in Latine by Ammianus Marcellinus: Now translated newly into English. Whereunto is annexed the Chronologie serving in stead of a briefe supplement of these former 13 Bookes, which by the iniurie of Time are lost: Together with compendious Annotations and Coniectures upon such hard places as occure in the said Historie, 1609.

and hated contention as a serpent; and his life so innocent that he never was all his days, either plaintiff or defendant in any suit at law in any court (tho' he suffered sometimes by it). As a scholar he was a reserved man, most indefatigable in his study, saying often, that there was no greater burden and enemy to him than idleness.[1]

Such facts are the soul of biography, and create for us the man whose work forms a fitting climax to this study of the Elizabethan art of translating. Holland came late to his true vocation. It was not until 1600, at the age of forty-eight, that he offered to Queen Elizabeth "the first fruits of a few-yeers studie,"[2] the vast folio of Livy's *Romane Historie*. After that he was indeed indefatigable. The equally vast labor of Pliny's *Naturall Historie*[3] appeared the very next year, and Plutarch's *Morals*[4] was inscribed to James in 1603. Then followed the *Suetonius*[5] (1606); next, *The Romane Historie* of Ammianus Marcellinus (1609); and, finally, Xenophon's *Cyrupaedia*,[6] completed in 1621, but not published until

[1] A. Wood, *Fasti Oxonienses*, ed. P. Bliss (London, 1815), I, 234.

[2] Dedication to *The Romane Historie* Written by T. Livius of Padua. Also, the Breviaries of L. Florus: with a Chronologie to the whole Historie: and the Topographie of Rome in old time, 1600.

[3] *The Historie of the World*. Commonly called The Naturall Historie of C. Plinius Secundus, 1601.

[4] *The Philosophie, commonlie called, The Morals*, Written by the learned Philosopher Plutarch of Chaeronea. Translated out of Greeke into English, and conferred with the Latin translations and the French . . . Whereunto are annexed the Summaries necessary to be read before every Treatise, 1603.

[5] *The Historie of Twelve Caesars, Emperours of Rome:* Written in Latine by C. Suetonius Tranquillus . . . Together with a Marginall Glosse, and other briefe Annotations there-upon, 1606.

[6] *Cyrupaedia, or the Institution and Life of Cyrus, King of Persians*, 1632.

1632 when it was prefaced by several commendatory verses (some of Thomas Heywood's among them), by the first printed account of the famous legendary pen, and by the dedication to Charles I.

These were his classic labors. But he is also credited with a Latin version of Speed's geographical description, *The Theatre of the Empire of Great Britaine*, for Continental use; and with *Paralipomena*, a supplement to Thomasius' *Dictionarium* (1615). He even issued a revised edition of *The Schoole of Salernes Regiment of Health*, which contained "learned and judicious directions" for the preservation of man's life. Holland's task was the translation of Villanova's Latin commentary on this work, and it is to be hoped for the sake of his patients that the doctor did not place too great faith in its medieval nostrums. After his death, a Latin version of Bauderon's *French Pharmacopoeia* was dedicated to the College of Physicians by his son. The last work of the translator's hand was the statement to the reader [1] that he wrote at the age of eighty-five to correct the mistakes of the first edition of his translation of Camden's *Britain*, which had appeared twenty-six years before. At the head of this volume a poem, "In praise of the Translator," by Thomas Meriell, strikes the note of all of Holland's work:

> Camden unto the learned did discover,
> What Holland to the Whol-land doth recite.

[1] Inserted at the end of the second edition which made its appearance in 1637, "not without the industry and helpe of my onely Son H. H."

II

The translator was a thorough patriot. His lifelong desire was to be of service to his country. He had reflected on the classic maxim that happy are those who can either do such things as deserve to be written, or write such things as are worthy to be read. And he prefaced his *Pliny* by saying:

As for my selfe, since it is neither my hap nor hope to attaine to such perfection as to bring foorth somewhat of mine owne which may quit the pains of a reader; and much lesse to perform any action that might minister matter to a writer; and yet so farre bound unto my native countrey and the blessed state wherein I have lived, as to render an account of my yeers passed & studies employed, during this long time of peace and tranquilitie, wherein (under the most gratious and happie government of a peerelesse Princesse, assisted with so prudent, politique, and learned Counsell) [1] all good literature hath had free progresse and flourished, in no age so much: me thought I owed this dutie, to leave for my part also (after many others) some small memoriall, that might give testimonie another day what fruits generally this peaceable age of ours hath produced. Endeavoured I have therefore to stand in this third ranke, and bestowed those hours which might be spared from the practise of my profession, and the necessarie cares of this life, to satisfie my countreymen now living, and to gratifie the age ensuing, in this kind.

Holland stands in the third rank, but it is a rank of which he was proud. The words with which he dedicated

---

[1] The *Pliny* was dedicated "to the Right Honourable Sir Robert Cecil, Knight, Principall Secretarie to the Queens Maiestie, Master of the Court of Wards and Liveries, Chancellor of the Universitie of Cambridge, and one of her Maiesties most Honourable privie Councell."

his *Livy* to the queen might be those of a voyager about
to set sail for the hazardous passage to America. His
attempt, he confesses, considering his imperfections, is
"venturous and overbold." For it is an enterprise "right
hard and exposed to perill." Not only Drake and the
traders, but he too brings wealth to his countrymen,
matters "not appropriat to the learned only, but acco-
modat to the rude paisant of the countrey; fitted for the
painefull artizan in town and citie; pertinent to the
bodily health of man, woman, and child; and in one
woord, suiting with all sorts of people living in a societie
and common-weale." [1] Such treasures does the *Pliny*
hold. His *Historie of the World* portrays "even Nature
her selfe, the immediat mother and nource of all things
under the Almightie." How earnestly Holland believed
in the wide importance of these translations appears perhaps even more clearly in the less fulsome language of his
preface to the *Livy*, where he states that he has a desire to perform "that which is profitable to the most,
namely, an english Historie of that C.[ommon] W.[ealth]
which of all others (if I have any judgement) affourdeth
most plenteous examples of devout zeale in their kind,
of wisedome, pollicie, iustice, valour, and all vertues
whatsoever."

This is the full flowering of the cardinal belief of the
sixteenth-century humanists: that the great classics of
Greece and Rome were to be read for their ethical values.

[1] *Pliny*, "The Preface to the Reader."

Neither Cheke nor, fifty years after him, Holland found any difficulty in inculcating Christian morality through the study of pagan writers. Holland's enthusiasm for Plutarch was so great that he wrote at the head of the opening section, "Of the Nouriture and Education of Children," the following justification against any possible detractors:

Now, albeit Plutarch (as a meere Pagane) hath both in this booke and also in others ensuing, where he treateth of vertues and vices, left out the chiefe and principall thing, to wit, the Law of God and his Trueth (wherein he was altogether ignorant), yet neverthelesse, these excellent precepts by him deliuered like raies which proceed from the light of nature remaining still in the spirit and soule of man,

not only "leave sinners inexcusable," but "shew how happie they be, who are guided by the heavenly light of holy Scripture."

Holland had not considered this matter lightly. For in recommending Pliny to his countrymen, he had previously admitted one scruple which at first had troubled him a little:

In attributing so much unto Nature, Plinie seemed to derogat from the almightie God, to him ἄγνωστος; and therefore daungerous (saith one) to be divulged. Farre be it from me, that I should publish any thing to corrupt men's manners, and much lesse to preiudice Christian religion.[1]

Therefore he first conferred "with sundrie divines about this point," and prints the reassuring letter of one of

[1] "The Preface to the Reader."

them, "Your loving friend in the Lord, H. F.," who
gives him high praise for opening to his countrymen
"the treasurie of Nature: therein to see and to admire
the wisdome, power, and the goodness of the only true
God, the Framer of Nature."

There are other carpers who still raise the futile objection (which had been so rife against Wilson and
Cheke) that no translations should be made into the
vulgar tongue. For such insects Holland, the toiler for
his nation's welfare, has only scorn:

It is a shame (quoth one) that Livie speaketh English as
hee doth: Latinists onely are to be acquainted with him: As
who would say, the souldiour were to have recourse unto the
universitie for militarie skill and knowledge; or the schollar
to put on arms and pitch a campe. What, should Plinie (saith
another) bee read in English, and the mysteries couched in his
books divulged: as if the husbandman, the mason, carpenter,
goldsmith, painter, lapidarie, and engraver, with other arti-
ficers, were bound to seeke unto great clearks or linguists for
instructions in their severall arts. Certes, such Momi as these,
besides their blind and erroneous opinion, thinke not so hon-
ourably of their native countrey and mother tongue as they
ought: who if they were so well affected that way as they
should be, would wish rather and endeavour by all means to
triumph now over the Romans in subduing their literature
under the dent of the English pen, in requitall of the conquest
sometime over this Island, atchieved by the edge of their
sword.[1]

The translator is both voyager and captain. In the
service of his country he has taken possession of a whole
battalion of foreign books. The words of his prefaces are

[1] *Ibid.*

significant in foreshadowing the quality of the translations themselves. He is every inch a scholar, a distinction shared by few contemporaries in his craft, and certainly by none of the other three treated in this book.
But his writing is just as racy and direct as theirs: no
film of learning separates his personality and his words.
It had not been so very difficult to turn Castiglione and
Montaigne into Englishmen, for their books were an
expression of the very changes through which England
itself was passing. North, too, had been aided in his
phenomenal achievement by the fact that Amyot had
already made Plutarch almost a contemporary. But to
wrestle with numberless volumes of text and commen-
taries, to give not only accurate translations but to an-
notate and explain "sundry tearmes somewhat obscure," [1] to confer with Beroaldus and Casaubon [2] and
add indexes of the principal matters contained, to go
beyond the French and Tuscan translators and compile
eighty vast folio pages of chronology of the history of
Rome,[3] to accomplish all this and still to write with such

---

[1] "An Explanation of Sundry Tearmes somewhat obscure . . . in favour
of the unlearned Reader" is attached to the *Plutarch*. A preface to the second
tome of the *Pliny* states that "for as much as this second Tome treateth
most of Physicke," the translator has thought it well to prefix "a briefe
Catalogue of such woords of Art."

[2] The preface to the readers of the *Suetonius* states that the annotations
are "out of mine owne readings, together with the select observations of
Beroaldus, Sabellicus, Torrentius and Casaubonus."

[3] "A Chronologie to the Historie of T. Livius, compiled according to the
Tables and Records of Verrius Flaccus in the Capitoll, and set out with most
profitable notes, shewing the varietie and disagreement of Authors about the
names of the Romane Consuls," fills pp. 1265–1345 of the *Livy*.

freshness that the translation seems an original, is not a
feat within the grasp of many scholars.

The secret of Holland's success lies in the fact that
what he read became part of his life. Livy and Suetonius
were not ancient classics, but men with something to say
that might be vital to England's destiny. They were not
to be laid up on shelves and studied, but to be read as
eagerly as one would talk on matters of importance with
one's fellow townsmen. In the sixteenth and early-
seventeenth centuries in England the classical past became so vivid that it seemed to some minds almost more
real than the present. For this reason Holland could say
that "the friendly acceptance which T. Livius of Padua
hath found in this Realme, since time he shewed himselfe in English weed unto her sacred Majestie, hath
trained over unto him his neighbour Plinius Secundus
from Verona." [1] It was natural for Holland to speak of
these books as though they were flesh and blood, since
they contained for him an essence as rich as life itself.
He had presented Livy to his queen in the way he might
have presented a distinguished foreigner:

Reach forth your gracious hand to T. Livius: who having
arrived long since & conversed as a meere stranger in this
your famous Iland, & now for love thereof learned in some
sort the language, humbly craveth your Majesties favour, to
be ranged with other free denizens of that kind: so long to live
under your princely protection, as hee shall duly keepe his
owne allegeance, and acquaint your liege subjects with reli-

---

[1] *Pliny*, "Dedication."

gious devotion after his manner, with wisdome, pollicie, vertue, valour, loyaltie, and not otherwise.

Holland's purpose, as he stated it in the *Pliny*, was especially "to profit and pleasure the most ignorant." [1] But he also had a strict belief in faithfulness to his original, from which he did not swerve. Horror at Nero's obscenity might make him write a footnote that he wished that Suetonius "had in this place and such like been altogether silent"; [2] but he gave the account, word for word. He made the fullest statement of his method in the *Livy*, and as the bulk of these pages is to be taken up with that work, it is well to turn to it now.

III

The translator proposed to himself what he calls Livy's own "warie circumspection" [3] in the task of translating him. He endeavored that his author should "deliver his mind in English, if not so eloquently by many degrees, yet as truly as in Latine." [4] To this end he compared other translations (which he had "some little skill in") with the chief Latin editions,[5] in order to

---

[1] In the preface to the second tome.

[2] *Suetonius*, p. 192.

[3] In the preface. This term strikes the modern reader as scarcely apt in view of Livy's wholly uncritical use of his sources.

[4] The preface to the index, p. 1404.

[5] Alfred Schäfer, *Die volkstümliche Liviusübersetzung Philemon Holland's* (Burgstädt, 1910), p. 19, sums up thus the question of what texts Holland used: "Aus seinen Worten ('To the Reader' S. 1234) geht klar hervor, dass er über die Schicksale der Liviusfragmente genau Bescheid gewusst hat. . . . In seiner Liviusübersetzung (S. 1171B) gibt er uns Sigonius als eine seiner Vor-

come as near as he possibly could "to the true meaning
of the Author." The guiding principle in this attempt
was to frame his pen "not to any affected phrase, but to
a meane and popular stile. Wherein, if I have called
againe into use some old words" — it is the glowing
patriot who speaks now — "let it be attributed to the
love of my countrey language: if the sentence be not so
concise, couched and knit togither, as the originall, loth
I was to be obscure and darke: have I not englished
everie word aptly?"[1]

Holland knew the extent of his labors. He knew the
rare qualities of his style. And so he was secure when he
turned to his critics: "Have I varied in some places from
the French or Italian? Censured I looke to be, and haply
reprooved: but like as Alcibiades said to one, πάταξον
οὖν καὶ ἄκουσον, i. *Strike hardly (Euribiades) so you
heare me speake*: even so say I; Find fault and spare not;
but withal, read the original better before ye give sentence." Hardly a man in the whole of England could
read the original better, and the learned doctor was
aware of it. He ended his long preface on the same note

---

lagen ausdrücklich an. Dass er diesen benutzt hat, beweisen auch die nach
dessen Text gemachten Ergänzungen XLII 40, 4 = 1138 H, 5–8; XLIV 24, 7
= 1185 D,8 (vgl. dazu die Anm. in der Ausg. von Weissenborn-Müller, Berlin,
1879 ff.). So darf man annehmen, dass H. ein ziemlich guter lateinischer Text
— vollständig bis auf eine grosse Lücke: XXXIII 1–17, 6 fehlt bei Holland
mit dem Bemerken: 'The beginning is not extant in the Latine' — vorge-
legen hat, eine Annahme, die der Verfasser bei seiner Vergleichung mit der
Liviusausgab, von Weissenborn-Müller unter Berücksichtigung der dort
verzeichneten textkritischen Bemerkungen bestätigt gefunden hat."

[1] The preface.

in which he dedicated the work to the queen: "And howsoever I have faulted otherwise by oversight, set against it my affection & desire to do some good whiles I live to my sweet native country." Thus he recommended unto his countrymen Livy in English habit, Livy who had

long been desirous to crosse the seas into this noble Iland, not as a travailer to soiourne for a time, in the Court onely or the Universities; but to remaine here still both in citie and countrey, and thereto hath learned our language indifferently; let it now appeare that this nation of ours (like to reap as great fruit and benefit by his acquaintance as any other) is readie also to receive and embrace him as friendly as the rest.

Livy was not remote from the Elizabethan spirit. His moral interpretation of history, his belief that Rome had grown to her greatness through the high virtues of her people, were firmly embedded in Englishmen's hearts. Here was a book that showed them the course their own people must follow. Consequently, if Holland did his work well, he was sure to be read. The first thing for him to master was the fundamental difference between the two languages. The compactness of the Latin cannot be reproduced: Livy could strip his expression to its essentials and depend on the inflected endings to convey his meaning, but the structure of English demands much greater fullness. In a long, involved sentence where the original had suddenly referred "ad eam rem," [1] it becomes necessary for Holland

[1] *Titi Livi ab urbe condita libri*, Book V, chap. 50, sec. 4. All references are to the edition of Weissenborn-Müller (Berlin, 1879 ff.).

to write "for the celebration of those plaies." [1] Since
ease for his reader is the first demand, the constant expansion of such phrases is inevitable. The sense must be
explicit, so where Livy wrote "ordines",[2] Holland translates "the ranks *of the enemies*." [3] "Duces" [4] is too
vague and is rendered as "the generals *on both sides*." [5]
The identity of the two parties of a conversation is made
unmistakable: "Tum dictator silentio facto, 'utinam,'
inquit" [6] becomes "Then after silence made, Would to
God (quoth the Dictatour *unto Manlius*)." [7] In like
manner, words of a general sense are limited by Holland
according to the context. Where Livy had written
simply "fortuna tum urbis," [8] he translates "when the
hard estate of the cittie"; [9] and "quae acta Romae" [10]
becomes "in what *bad* tearmes all things stood at
Rome." [11]

The steady desire for clarity causes him to define a
purpose where Livy had left it implied: "went up into
the pulpit *to make an Oration unto them*" [12] for "in con-
tionem escendit"; [13] "and with twelve forked stakes a
peece, *for to pitch in the rampart*" [14] for "vallisque duo-
denis." [15] But Holland's determination to be clear does
not stop with the introduction of explanatory words; it
affects the whole structure of his prose. To bind together

[1] Holland, *Livy*, p. 211 F. (The folio pages are divided into lettered
sections of ten lines each.)

[2] VI 13, 3.   [3] p. 225 B.   [4] I 23, 7.   [5] p. 16 L.
[6] VI 15, 4.   [7] p. 226 L.   [8] II 12, 4.   [9] p. 51 E.
[10] III 50, 12.   [11] p. 121 D.   [12] p. 48 L.
[13] II 7, 7.   [14] p. 106 I.   [15] III 27, 3.

the long, flowing periods he constantly makes the con-
necting links stronger. "Ad ea" [1] becomes "to these
challenges and imputations," [2] a simple "haec" [3] is
written as "these and such like remonstrances," [4] and
"adversus ea" [5] is transformed into "but (all these big
words notwithstanding)." [6] This tendency is one of the
translator's chief characteristics. He not only instinctively strengthens connectives: he introduces several of
his own. A favorite phrase to bind his meaning is: "but
now to returne." "But now to returne. Things passing
thus (as I said before) the Consuls abovenamed . . .
entred their government" [7] appears for "His rebus
actis consules ii, quos diximus . . . magistratum occe-
pere"; [8] "But to returne againe to Scipio: When he had
called forth the hostages" [9] for the brief "ceterum voca-
tis obsidibus." [10]

This strengthening of connectives is most effectual
when Holland sums up a whole series of statements and
knits them together into a unity. Sometimes he inserts
a clause at the beginning of a passage to define its trend:

Postero die singulis captivis ab equite ac centurione sorte ductis et, quorum eximia virtus fuerat, binis, aliis sub corona venundatis . . . IV 34, 4.	The morrow after, *the Dicta-tor disposed of his prisoners thus,* He drew them by lot, and gave to every horseman and Centu-rion one, and to as many as had done more valiantly than other, two apeece; the rest he sold in portsale . . . 161 E.

[1] XLII 41, 1. [2] p. 1138 L. [3] III 10, 14. [4] p. 95 C.
[5] VI 38, 8. [6] p. 244 H. [7] p. 163 B.
[8] IV 37, 3. [9] p. 622 M. [10] XXVI 49, 7.

Again, he introduces a whole sentence into the middle of a long speech to mark the important fact: "*But as to the substance of the matter, this was the point: namelie,* that the people of Rome were not under the regiment of a king, but were a free state" [1] for "Non in regno populum Romanum, sed in libertate esse." [2] How subtle and effective this device of the translator can be is seen when he sums up an extended series of details by a phrase suggesting the quality of them all, as, for example:

There the Tribunes Militarie without getting aforehand a convenient place to pitch their tentes in, without fortifying the same with any trench or rampiers . . . even without any regard of God . . . without Auspices and bird-tokens, without reconciliation to God by sacrifice, *full unhappily and in ill houre*, ranged their battell.[3]

Such workmanship shows Holland's complete realization of the extent to which he must transform the Latin if he is to profit and pleasure the more ignorant. But all his additions are not determined by the demands of clarity and the structure of the language. He delights in throwing simple statements of fact into the form of an elaborate summary, thus: "When he had received the Senats decree *to this effect: Imprimis,* That Camillus should be called back again out of exile by a Ward-leet, or the suffrages of the Curia: *Item,* that by the voices of

[1] p. 54 H.
[2] II 15, 3.
[3] p. 204 H–I (Livy, V 38, 1).

the people he should be created Dictator out of hand." [1]
He delights also in a fullness of expression which never
adds unwarrantably to the text but gives the idea new
color. "But from these their folkemotes, never came
there any of you home to his house, richer of *one gray
groat or single denier*" [2] is surely a rich version of the
statement "Sed ex illis contionibus numquam vestrum
quisquam re . . . domum auctior rediit." [3]

This striking love of fullness and elaboration is the
chief cause why elements of contrast, left implied by
Livy, are always brought out by Holland. "But in
truth, these new dessignements and plots of Manlius,
rather than the warre, forced the Senate to create a Dictatour" [4] appears for "Sed nova consilia Manli magis
conpulere senatum ad dictatorem creandum"; [5] "under
no meane person *but an excellent* maister, *even king
Ancus* himselfe" [6] for "sub haud paenitendo magistro." [7]
Sometimes the original contained not even an implied
contrast, as when the bare statement "Apparere nihil
sinceri esse" [8] is expanded to "Surely there is no sound-

---

[1] p. 209 E ("Accepto inde senatus consulto, ubi comitiis curiatis revo-
catus de exilio iussu populi Camillus dictator extemplo diceretur," V 46, 10).
This device is very common in Holland, as in such an extended passage as:
"*Imprimis*, that all the temples . . . should bee repaired . . . *Item*, that the
manner of cleansing them should be searched . . . *Moreover*, that with the
inhabitants of Caere, there should be made a league . . . *Item*, That there
should be set out the Plaies called Capitolini . . . And that M. Furius should
ordain a guild . . . *Finally*, to the end there should be also some satisfaction
& expiation made of that night voice," p. 211 E–F (Livy, V 50, 2–5).

[2] p. 134 L.   [3] III 68, 4.   [4] p. 224 H.   [5] VI 11, 10.
[6] p. 26 K.   [7] I 35, 5.   [8] III 35, 6.

nesse *nor goodnesse* herein, *but all meere dissimulation and hypocrisie.*" [1] More often, however, Holland elaborates an already existing contrast in Livy, or pitches its phrasing more sharply, as in the addition to "Ignosci adulescentibus posse, senibus non posse," [2] of a stinging phrase, "Youths indeed might well be pardoned, but *such old babes* as they might not." [3]

There is another way, quite similar, by which Holland adds to the original. Where Livy gave the result of an action, Holland often lives through the series of events leading up to this result, thus: "*Then came* the consuls *forth, tooke their places* and set them downe on the tribunall seat" [4] for "Consules in sedem processere suam." [5] And the far more extended: "Whereupon the people ran together, *and made a roiot, grew to words, and from words to brawles, insomuch as they went together by the eares,* and made a fray in manner of a battell," [6] which represents the brief "Concursu hominum rixa ac prope proelium fuit." [7] A variant of this practice occurs where Livy stated the fact, and Holland elaborates the reasons. The Romans "remembred wel enough, that their forefathers were not under shade *for feare of sunburning*, nor had their houses over their heads *for taking cold*, when they first created and ordeined that magistracie of Tribunes" [8] is the translation for "meminisse hanc ipsam

[1] pp. 110 M–111 A.
[2] II 18, 10.
[3] p. 56 G.
[4] p. 47 B.
[5] II 5, 8.
[6] p. 55 C–D.
[7] II 18, 2.
[8] p. 183 C.

potestatem non in umbra nec in tectis maiores suos creasse." [1]   It loses no vividness through its explicit details.

Holland "englished" every word aptly, but he did not attempt a mirror-like copy of the original. His prime consideration was to have the book read by the people; his desire for "a mean and popular style" led him into the main highway of his native speech. He possessed the love of doublets that we have traced through the other Elizabethan translators. Nouns are doubled: "storme and tempest," [2] "in audacitie and boldnesse," [3] "more for thy dishonestie and shame." [4]   So are adjectives: "meet and decent," [5] "a forward and valorous knight." [6] So are verbs: "whipped and scourged," [7] "overtoiled and wearied," [8] "cherish and foster," [9] "confounded and overthrowne." [10]   In some instances this increasing of words is more extensive, as when eight adjectives appear in place of two, "those to whome *God and* nature hath given bodies more big *and corpulent than strong and able*, hearts *more stout and courageous* than constant *and*

[1] V 6, 5.

[2] p. 168 G ("tempestatem," IV 44, 9).

[3] p. 32 M ("audacia," I 46, 6).

[4] p. 70 L ("tibi turpius," II 40, 8).

[5] p. 99 D ("decuit," III 17, 5).

[6] p. 32 M (Here, as not infrequently, there is no adjective in the Latin, but the single word "virum," I 46, 6).

[7] p. 318 H ("virgis caesos," IX 9, 2).

[8] p. 413 B ("fessis," XXI 35, 6).

[9] p. 28 K ("nutriamus," I 39, 4).

[10] p. 230 L ("opprimi," VI 20, 3).

resolute" [1] for "cui natura corpora animosque magna magis quam firma dederit." [2] Occasionally words are relished for their own sake: "The Gaules stood upon the banke with *dissant* [3] hooping, *hollaing, yelling,* and singing after their manner." [4] And sometimes this relish betrays Holland into overloading his prose. The heavy length of the expression that "his vertues now were in their growth, flourished, and grew ripe unto perfection" [5] is useless when compared with the concise "maturescente virtute." [6] The extra words in "Wo worth men conquered, and downe with them still" [7] eliminate the poignancy of the cry, "Vae victis." [8]

But there are few such instances. If Holland's weighty periods are remote from the simplicity of the Bible, they are equally remote from any of Florio's fads. His use of the tricks of euphuism is most sparing. His occasional alliteration is very effective, as in "So sweete and savorie it is" [9] for "Tanta dulcedo est"; [10] or in the recommendation to the vestal virgin that she should be "in her raiment . . . not so deft as devout, and weare her garments rather sainctly than sightly," [11] where the clause is also doubled to give the swing of the parallel construction. Play on the sound of words appears now

[1] p. 208 H. [2] V 44, 4.
[3] Misprint for "distant" or perhaps "dissonant."
[4] p. 408 K ("Galli occursant in ripa cum variis ululatibus cantuque moris sui," XXI 28, 1).
[5] p. 96 L. [6] III 12, 7. [7] p. 211 A.
[8] V 48, 9. [9] p. 247 E. [10] VI 41, 11.
[11] p. 168 I ("colique *s*ancte potius quam *s*cite iussit," IV 44, 12).

and then: a certain situation demands that a consul "be not onely the enformer, but also the reformer."[1] But alliteration is generally limited to such popular expressions[2] as "to heaven nor hell," "pent up and pinned," "to store and stocke," "before any stroke strucken," "through thike and thinne," "thike and threefold," "witting and willing"; and the use of words that jingle is confined to "pell-mell," "will they, nil they," "tag and rag."

Holland's diction flowed in the main channel of contemporary usage. The desire to use the native English stock of words did not betray him into obscure archaisms. He rarely introduced any word that is not still perfectly comprehensible today.[3] He did not come too late to profit from the Elizabethan freedom of com-

---

[1] p. 148 M (The Latin nouns are "auctorem," "vindicem," IV 13, 10).

[2] These are so frequent that they do not require notes.

[3] Occasionally he fastened upon a strange word such as "a presaging osse." This became a favorite with him, and he gave it this learned defense: "For want of a proper tearme to expresse the Latine (Omen) all translators hitherto, French, Italian, and English, have been put to their shifts, and helpe themselves with (Presage) . . . Whereas that other word (Osse) is very significant, and in analogie aequivalent to (Omen). I mervell much therefore, why it is thought either strange and new (seeing it is English, used no doubt commonly in times past, and at this day current in the North-parts, where the people haply are more observant of such presages) rather than many other forraine words, brought into our language, and raunged with the English: or why it should be condemned as absonant and not pleasing to the eare, more than ὄσσα in Greek . . . From whence, who seeth not that (Osse and Osing both) are derived?" p. 1107 C–D. The *New English Dictionary* states that this word is not found before Holland as a noun, although it exists as a verb in the fourteenth century West Midland dialect. It could not have come from the Greek "without many intermediate links, of which in this case none are found."

pounding, to be able to write of "that night voice . . .
the fore-messenger and warning-giver of their destruc-
tion." [1] He benefited to the full from the French and
Spanish importations that were passing current in his
time: he speaks of "the Consuls Sentinels, his corps de
gard," [2] "the oiez" of the public crier,[3] "the Rendez-
vous" of an army,[4] "the Burgeoises or cittizens" [5] of
Rome, "the Carthaginian Armadoes," [6] of such a one
who "made a prowd bravado and shew of his strength,"[7]
of another who "deserveth the bastanado, to be drie
beaten and well cudgeled." [8] Nor does he fail to employ
common Latin phrases — some of which do not happen
to appear in the passage he is translating, but serve his
purpose none the less: "Thus men commonly talked pro
et contra," [9] "gratis and without raunsome," [10] "not
soundly and bona fide." [11]

A distinguishing feature of Holland's prose is his free
introduction of metaphors. Sometimes these are drawn
from nature. He writes of the forced sale of Manlius'
land "which was the chiefe and capitall Manour of his
inheritance, *even the fairest flower of his garland*"; [12] or he
develops an analogy to a fruitless harvest: "I feare mee,
that even this present so goodly a shew of ranckenesse
as it maketh now, *will run up all to straw, and beare no*

---

[1] p. 212 G.   [2] p. 157 A.   [3] p. 304 G.   [4] p. 173 E.
[5] p. 246 G.   [6] p. 440 K.   [7] p. 233 B.   [8] p. 183 E.
[9] p. 1016 G ("haec agitata sermonibus," XXXVIII 50, 10).
[10] p. 633 C.   [11] p. 830 H ("nec . . . cum fide," XXXII 33, 10).
[12] p. 226 H ("caput patrimonii," VI 14, 10).

head to yeeld corne in the end." [1] Sometimes the metaphors are taken from the activities of men in order to illuminate a general statement with a specific detail: "But the name of the Fabij, the Fabij I say, passed all the rest *and won the spurs.*" [2] The translator also makes an amazingly skillful use of personification of the sort that gives life to inanimate objects. He tells how "the Acts & Ordinances . . . lay a long time *asleepe in the deck*, and nothing done." [3] He speaks of a State that "*lying a bleeding*, had utterly perisht." [4] He makes a Senator promise the people prosperity "so long as the cittie standeth *on foot, and holdeth up the head.*" [5]

The style resulting from all these tendencies is strongly figurative. Holland brings in an image whereever possible: "varios vultus" [6] are called "an alphabet of faces," [7] "autumno" [8] is translated as "in the fall of the leafe." [9] When he wants to express the fact that both armies were eager for a battle, he says: "They were sharpe set, *and their fingers itched* on both sides to be a fighting." [10] Concrete words are substituted for abstract: Ascanius was not old enough to rule the empire,

---

[1] p. 481 C–D (The Latin is a straight statement of fact: "Vereor, ne haec quoque laetitia luxuriet nobis ac vana evadat," XXIII 12, 12).

[2] p. 75 C ("Fabium nomen, Fabia gens maxime enituit," II 45, 16).

[3] p. 172 K ("iacere tam diu inritas actiones," IV 51, 4).

[4] p. 91 B ("venissetque in periculum," III 5, 8).

[5] p. 611 F ("res publica incolumis," XXVI 36, 9).

[6] XXII 7, 12.　　　　[7] p. 436 I.

[8] V 6, 2.　　　　[9] p. 183 B.

[10] p. 504 L ("Utraque pars avidi certaminis erant," XXIII 44, 6).

"nondum maturus imperio," [1] which Holland translates "Now was not Ascanius, Aeneas his sonne, ripe as
yet for age *to sway the scepter*." [2] In this way both "im-
perium" and "regnum" are nearly always expressed
figuratively as "a crowne and scepter" or "the roiall
crowne." The bare statement "Vires non experientur" [3]
is given color thus: "But never will they feele your fists,
and trie how keene your swords be." [4] The general reference is made individual: "aliquis" [5] becomes "some
odde groome"; [6] a wrong so great that it would have
disturbed even the mildest natured is said to have "been
ynough to have mooved a very Saint." [7]

Holland's love of the specific is absolute. Where Livy
had written "signo dato," [8] he translates "at sound of
trumpet." [9] He states the materials of which substances
are made: "tabula" [10] is "a table of brasse," [11] "torque
spoliavit" [12] is written, he "despoiled him of his collar *of
gold*." [13] He instinctively gives added details: "by casting *morsels of bread* and victuals" [14] for "ciboque obi-
ciendo," [15] "by *dint of* steele, and not by *weight of* gold to
redeem their countrie" [16] for "ferroque, non auro recu-

[1] I 3, 1.   [2] p. 4 H.
[3] IV 5, 5.   [4] p. 143 B.
[5] "Deinde, cum aliquis omissa verecundia quempiam nominasset,"
XXIII 3, 10.
[6] "Afterwards, when some odde groome past all shame and reverence,
seemed to nominate one," p. 474 L.
[7] p. 118 G (Livy, III 45, 6).
[8] V 43, 2.   [9] p. 207 D.   [10] VI 29, 9.
[11] p. 238 G.   [12] VI 42, 6.   [13] p. 248 H.
[14] p. 150 G.   [15] IV 15, 6.   [16] p. 211 B.

perare patriam." [1] Caught by the pictorial aspect of a situation, he quickly transforms a Roman town into his own Coventry's image: Camillus entered the town, and saw

the dores standing open, the shop *windowes* up, all kinde of wares set out to sale *upon the bulkes:* the Crafts-men *and Artisans* busily every one occupied at his worke: the *Grammer*-schooles ringing againe with a *chirme* of schollers, learning *and saying their lessons:* the streetes full of women and children amongst the other common people going too & fro. [2]

Such details are not necessary, but they make vivid prose. To say that "the bootie thereof came unto the Questors *coffers*" [3] instead of "ad quaestores," [4] or "with their haire hanging *loose about their shoulders*" [5] instead of "crinibus passis," [6] gives an added range to the imagination. There is an angry strength in "Hang him *by the necke, and strangle him* upon a cursed tree" [7] which is not found in "Arbore infelici suspende." [8] And often a simple word of description brings to the sentence a wholly new life: "after some *hoat* words" [9] for "pauca ... vociferatus," [10] "lying on the *hard and bare* ground" [11] for "humi iacentem," [12] "*this beardlesse* boy" [13] for

---

[1] V 49, 3.

[2] p. 235 B–C ("Ingressus urbem ubi patentes ianuas et tabernis apertis proposita omnia in medio vidit intentosque opifices suo quemque operi et ludos litterarum strepere discentium vocibus ac repletas semitas inter vulgus aliud puerorum et mulierum huc atque illuc euntium," VI 25, 9).

[3] p. 197 D.	[4] V 26, 8.	[5] p. 10 K.
[6] I 13, 1.	[7] p. 19 D–E.	[8] I 26, 11.
[9] p. 140 G.	[10] IV 1, 6.	[11] p. 395 D.
[12] XXI 4, 7.	[13] p. 399 A–B.	

"puer." [1] The majesty of this detail can be fully appreciated only from a longer passage. Take part of the famous section about Horatius at the bridge: much of the elaboration, many of the doublets, are not in the least essential, but the whole is powerful and vibrant:

Vadit inde in primum aditum pontis, insignisque inter conspecta cedentium pugnae terga obversis comminus ad ineundum proelium armis ipso miraculo audaciae obstupefecit hostis ... Circumferens inde truces minaciter oculos ad proceres Etruscorum nunc singulos provocere, nunc increpare omnes: servitia regum superborum ... Quae cum in obiecto cuncta scuto haesissent, neque ille minus obstinatus ingenti pontem obtineret gradu. — II 10, 5–10.

Then advanceth he himselfe unto the first entrie *or foot* of the bridge, and *all* goodly to bee seene, amongst those that *would no point* fight, but shewed their backes, he so bent *his sword and target in their verie faces*, resolute to encounter with them hand to hand, that even with his wonderfull *hardiness and incredible* courage, he astonied *& amazed* his enemies ... Then casting *all* about in menacing manner his *fierie and* terrible eies, towards the *captaines and* principals of the Tuskanes, one while he chalenged them *one by one* to single fight: otherwhiles he rated them all *in general, calling them the hirelings and* slaves of proud kings *and tyrants* ... All this while bare he off *their shot which light* upon his target, and there stucke, *and nath'lesse with full resolution* kept the bridge still, *walking his stations, and staulking like a giant.*" — p. 50 I–M.

The love of striking words sometimes betrays Holland into extravagant speech. It is a shock to read, in the description of Hannibal's army crossing the Alps, that the

[1] XXI 10, 8.

soldiers had to go through "the slabberie snow-broth, as it relented and melted about their heeles." [1] But usually the translation is even: throughout the volume raciness has taken the place of dignity. "The Nobles were wont with much heave and shove to fill but three rowmes." [2] The Senators of Rome are "strucken into their dumpes"; [3] the Tribunes "made but a tush thereat." [4] The Senate and Commons are "at jarre and together by the eares." [5] There is no equivalent for the quality of such phrases in the original, and often, especially in the passages of conversation, they are extraordinarily vigorous. For instance, "But now, seeing a Senatour bluntly spurreth me to the question" [6] takes the place of the plain "nunc interroganti senatori." [7]

Further than this, Holland lends a wholly English flavor to the book by using many favorite colloquial phrases: "But might prevailed more than right," [8] "Every man should be his own carver," [9] the Tribunes "raigned . . . and ruled the rost," [10] "This seemed to bee a bone cast betweene the Nobles and the Commons, to set them together at strife and contention," [11] "their

---

[1] p. 413 E ("fluentemque tabem liquescentis nivis," XXI 36, 6).

[2] p. 180 L ("Trina loca cum contentione summa patricios explere solitos," V 2, 10).

[3] p. 245 D ("Stupor silentiumque inde ceteros patrum defixisset," VI 40, 1).

[4] p. 244 H ("adversus ea cum contemptim tribuni plebis," VI 38, 8).

[5] p. 236 M–237 A ("Patres ac plebem in semet ipsos versos," VI 28, 1).

[6] p. 481 B.   [7] XXIII 12, 9.

[8] p. 145 F.   [9] p. 193 E.

[10] p. 101 A–B.   [11] p. 170 H.

teeth a watering," [1] "one foot already in the grave," [2]
"not one jot," [3] "a world of discords & troubles." [4]
Sometimes these render a straightforward Latin phrase,
as "for oftentimes in the twinckling of an eie, & in the
very turning of an hand" [5] for "puncto saepe temporis " ; [6] at others they are based on nothing in the
original: "He would leave his Infanterie behind him
at sixe and seven" [7] for "relicto peditatu omni." [8] In
every case they bring the Latin classic just so much
closer to the English reader. [9] And even more effective
for this purpose is the constant interjection into the
speeches of such phrases as "nay," "yea marry," "no,
no," "tush," "ywis," "yea verily."

In still another way the book is put into modern dress.
For when the contents of "certaine propheticall verses
of one Martius" are stated in Livy's prose, Holland
brings them into the vogue of his day by turning them
into fairly deft verse:

> From Trojane line, O Romane once descended,
> Flie Canna river, neere to Cannae towne:
> Least strangers borne, who have thy death intended,
> Force thee to fight on Diomede his downe.
> But warning mine, thou wilt not rest upon,

[1] p. 138 H.   [2] p. 137 E.   [3] p. 94 L.
[4] p. 166 L.   [5] p. 106 K–L.   [6] III 27, 8.
[7] p. 459 C–D.   [8] XXII 43, 4.

[9] Colloquial phrases of this sort are so numerous as to be perhaps the most
outstanding element in Holland's style. Among others are: "broken the
yce," "tooth and naile," "hand over head, and at a venture," "left in the
lurch," "from hand to mouth," "broken to fitters," "laid their heads together," "took him in hand." The two last are particularly frequent.

Untill with bloud thou first doe fill the plaine:
And then to sea from fruitfull land, anon
Thy men shall downe the streame by thousands slaine.
Thy flesh must bait the fish in Ocean deepe,
And lure the foules that flie from high to pray,
And feed wild beasts, on earth below that keepe.
Marke well my words. Jove thus me taught to say.[1]

The tabulation of what Holland did to Livy has suggested the qualities of his style. He writes with freshness and energy, but his prose is by no means purely colloquial. He employs the ornaments of rhetoric to give it weight, he increases the emphasis by doubling and repetition, and by an elaboration of the balanced sentence. Where the original had used one noun and one verb, he uses three of each: "A waightie burthen (quoth he) I see is imposed upon me by the people of Rome . . . a greater *charge is enjoined me* by the Senate . . . but the heaviest *lode* of all *is laid upon me* by the exceeding kindnesse and obsequious benignitie of these my honourable brethren and colleagues."[2] But his pages are not marred by arti-

---

[1] p. 555 A–B ("Amnen, Troiugena, fuge Cannam, ne te alienigenae cogant in campo Diomedis conserere manus. Sed neque credes tu mihi, donec compleris sanguine campum, multaque milia occisa tua deferet amnis in pontum magnum ex terra frugifera; piscibus atque avibus ferisque, quae incolunt terras, is fuat esca caro tua. Nam mihi ita Juppiter fatus est," XXV 12, 5–7). Another prophetical song which is recorded a few lines further down is turned by Holland into seven rhymed couplets, p. 555 C–D.

[2] p. 220 I ("Ingens inde ait onus a populo Romano sibi . . . magnum a senatu . . . maximum tam honorato collegarum obsequio iniungi," VI 6, 8–9). Repetition of an idea is made fairly effective in "Exercise your rigour *and crueltie, and spare not,* upon our backs and *sides in scourging us, yea* upon our necks *and heads also, in taking them from our shoulders:* so yee forbeare to assaile our chastitie *and honestie,*" p. 118 H–I, for "Saevite in tergum et in cervices nostras: pudicitia saltem in tuto sit," III 45, 9.

ficial devices. He does not always use the rigid, balanced construction even when it exists in the Latin.[1] He breaks up Livy's periods when they seem too long. And that ease means more to him than rhetoric is apparent from his great skill in introducing variety. In a short passage of a dozen lines about the auspices,[2] Livy had used the noun "auspicia" seven times, and the past participle "auspicato" three. Holland varies it thus: "of the solemnitie of the Auspices" (de ... auspiciis), "by the approbation of the gods, testified by flight of birds" (auspiciis), "by the same Auspices" (auspiciis), "these tokens and presages" (auspicia), "with regard of flight, sight and feeding of the birdes" (auspicato), "they" (auspicia), "by observation of the birds" (auspicato), "by means of the birdes" (auspicato), "by them" (auspicia), "these Auspicia" (auspicia).

One final characteristic detail of Holland's style is still to be noted. In his preface the translator spoke "of that Patheticall spirit of his [Livy's] in moving affections." Finding this element in his author, he has devoted himself to bringing it out to the full. His efforts in heightening the emotional pitch of the original can be shown simply by his repeated introduction of the adjec-

[1] For instance, "whiles the enemies soldiers were raw and untrained; and the better and wiser man of the two Generals was unmeet for service, by reason of his wound as yet uncured; and the courages of the Gaules lustie and froward," p. 423 E, where the Latin has the exact "dum ... dum ... dum" construction, XXI 53, 9.

[2] p. 247 B–C (Livy, VI 41, 4–7).

tive "poor": "and evermore the blame light upon *poore*
Caeso"; [1] "by turning out their *poore fellow* cittizens
into banishment, & sending them away, *God knowes
whither*"; [2] "for to comfort their *poore* hearts again"; [3]
and in the Alps passage: "*All that the poore garrons and
beasts* could do, was to tumble *and wallow* only, upon the
slipperie glassie yce, and the molten slabbie snow." [4]

But Holland goes beyond the mere introduction of adjectives in his efforts to increase the emotion. [5] Where
Livy wrote "Captum Aventinum conclamaverunt," [6]
he lets the actual sound of the cry be heard: "They ran
crying about the citie, The Aventine is taken, The Aventine is taken!" [7] There is a story-teller's phrase in the
statement "And before day they encountred together
(but *you must thinke* the moon shone all night)." [8] He
often creates a dramatic contrast, as in Cato's speech
against the mutinous sedition of women to gain equality
— the women who are "wringing out of your hands,
maugre your beards, the libertie of your voyces and suf-

---

[1] p. 96 H ("in unius Caesonis suspectum," III 11, 11).

[2] p. 95 B–C ("exilio et relegatione civium," III 10, 13).

[3] p. 172 L ("delenimentum animis," IV 51, 5).

[4] p. 413 E–F ("In levi tantum glacie tabidaque nive voluntabantur,"
XXI 36, 8).

[5] The way Holland builds up the parallel phrases of a sentence is also
often calculated to produce a more intense effect: "to the end that *sorrow
upon sorrow*, funerall upon funerall, *one mournefull death after another*, should
infortunately be heaped upon *our house &* familie, p. 616 K, for "ut aliud
super aliud cumularetur familiae nostrae funus," XXVI 41, 8.

[6] XXVI 10, 6.

[7] p. 590 I.

[8] p. 199 B–C (". . . sed luna pernox erat," V 28, 10).

frages." [1] The emotion of a speaker is sometimes exter-
nalized: in place of the simple "Hannibal peto pacem," [2]
Holland writes, "But now I, *even I, no worse a man than
Anniball*, do sue for peace." [3] And finally, a scornful
tone is emphasized, or a touch of irony is made more
biting. "What, *Sir*? How if *your Mastership* wil not put
up & prefer that which is commodious and profitable for
the people?" [4] carries a sharp sarcasm unknown in the
direct "Quid? si tu non tuleris quod commodum est
populo?" [5] And when Minucius is angry because Fabius
merely protects the army from a sudden attack by the
enemy and risks no battle himself, Holland lends a
pointed conclusion to his scorn: "And we here leade our
armie as if they were a flock of sheepe, over the shadowie
forests, and hils out of the way, hidden among the clouds
and thick woods *to keepe them from the heate of sunne*." [6]

IV

The analysis of the elements that compose Holland's
remarkable prose is illuminating, but it does not convey
the full extent of his work as translator. For beyond the
consideration of what words he should use lay the demands of his double purpose. He was determined both
to make the book easy for the reader, and to bring out

[1] p. 854 M ("ereptis suffragiis vestris," XXXIV 3, 9).
[2] XXX 30, 29.   [3] p. 761 E.
[4] p. 246 I.   [5] VI 40, 12.
[6] p. 440 L (Livy, XXII 14, 8).

its essential qualities to the full. To achieve both these results he faced the necessity of explaining whatever Roman terms and customs might be obscure to the unlettered.

Often doubling suffices to clarify the meaning of a name: "the Anciles *or heavenly shields*,"[1] "by Augurie or *flight of birds*,"[2] "Can a Pulvinar *be celebrated, or a sacred Table* be spred *and furnished* in any place, but in the Capitoll?"[3] Just as often, however, the translator feels it incumbent upon him to explain the purpose of a ceremony, to say: "The Romanes likewise upon that miraculous signe, *for the purging and expiation thereof*, celebrated solemne publicke sacrifices *for the space of nine daies*, called a Novendiall."[4] Or to specify the difference between the military decorations "murales" and "civici," he writes "amongst which were two goodly murall garlands *for scaling and entering upon the wals first*: eight civick coronets *for saving the lives of citizens in danger*."[5]

Sometimes it is a question of giving further information than that contained in the text, of telling his readers that "oraculum"[6] in a certain passage means "the oracle there of Apollo,"[7] and that "libris"[8] refers to

---

[1] p. 247 D.   [2] p. 6 H.   [3] p. 213 C.

[4] p. 22 M ("Romanis quoque ab eodem prodigio novendiale sacrum publice susceptum est," I 31, 4).

[5] p. 231 A ("in quibus insignes duas murales coronas, civicas octo," VI 20, 8).

[6] XXII 57, 5.   [7] p. 467 C.   [8] V 50, 3.

"the bookes of Sibylla." [1] Unfamiliar geography is made clear: "Trebia, Trasumennus, Cannae" [2] is rendered "the river Trebia, the mere Thrasymenus, the town Cannae." [3] In addition his pages include many of the elaborate explanations of the real scholar. When the Rostra is mentioned, he takes it upon himself to add in parenthesis: "A publick crosse (as it were) or pulpit in Rome, out of which the Magistrats made Orations to the people, beautified with the beakheads of ships and their brasen pikes, called Rostra." [4] But perhaps his greatest skill in this kind is shown in the subtle detail he uses in describing the Romans' clothes. The "toga praetexta" [5] is called "the royall purple robe embrodered, named Toga praetexta." [6] The "palmata tunica" [7] becomes "a coat wrought with needle worke, representing the Date tree." [8] Further, such a word as "toga" is given slightly different meanings according to its context. In one place it is called "his Senators robe"; [9] in another Cincinnatus, found by the Senate's messenger digging his ground, is requested to "put on his best gown"; [9] again, "the Consull . . . in his long robe and gowne of peace." [10]

Holland is thoroughly steeped in the lore of Rome, but he is aware of the cardinal fact that if his book is not to be for the learned alone, he must give it a contemporary

[1] p. 211 E. [2] XXVI 41, 11. [3] p. 616 L.
[4] p. 151 A. [5] I 8, 3. [6] p. 7 C.
[7] XXX 15, 11. [8] p. 750 K. [9] p. 106 G.
[10] p. 146 M.

flavor. So he sometimes writes "in their single doublet and hose" [1] for "cum singulis vestimentis." [2] He translates "Lusitani" [3] by "the Portugales," [4] and "Galli" [5] by "the Frenchmen." [6] When he comes to "post bellum Actiacum," [7] he brings the reference home to the popular mind, which had been fed by North's translation and several plays on the theme, by writing: "after the battell of Actium (with Antonius & Cleopatra)." [8] The extent to which he modernizes Roman customs to make them accord with their English equivalents can be seen in his handling of certain key-words, such as "patres," "plebs," "comitium," "curia," "praetor," "praetorium," "praefectus." "Patres et plebs" is generally turned into "Lords and Commons," sometimes into "Nobles and Commons." [9] "Comitium" varies with the context: "common hall" ("in their common hall, named Comitium"), [10] "hall," [11] "High court," [12] "Parlement," [13] "high court of parlement." [13] "Curia" is sometimes allowed to remain in the English, but is sometimes changed to "the Counsell house," [14] or again to "the Senate house." [15] The "praetor" becomes "the Lord chiefe Justice" [16] or the "L. Governour of the citie," [16] except at the times he is serving, not at Rome but in a province, when he is called "L. Deputie in Gallia." [16] Similarly the "prae-

[1] p. 146 K.	[2] IV 10, 4.	[3] XXXVII 46, 7.
[4] p. 972 I.	[5] V 53, 2.	[6] p. 214 H.
[7] I 19, 3.	[8] p. 14 I.	[9] p. 248 K.
[10] p. 51 A.	[11] p. 99 D.	[12] p. 167 C.
[13] p. 453 A.	[14] p. 34 H.	[15] p. 33 E.
[16] p. 452 L.		

torium" is "the Consuls Quarter," [1] "the Generall his
court"; [2] or when Carthaginian Hannibal is the speaker,
"in praetorio patris" [3] becomes "in the very tent and
roiall pavilion of my father." [4] The translation of
"praefectus" is varied perhaps still more in the effort to
naturalize his office in England. He becomes "Provost
marshall," [5] "the President of the Cittie," [6] "the Con-
stable of the castle," [7] in accordance with his duties in
each passage.

But beyond all scattered details there are one or two
principal ways to show how this Latin classic was made
English. Chief among them is Holland's treatment of
the Roman religious customs. For the very words he
chooses reveal the whole extent to which the English
Renaissance assimilated the pagan world. The translator's prime consideration here as elsewhere in his book
is to bridge the gap between antiquity and the present,
to make the past comprehensible to his readers. But the
differences between paganism and Christianity are so
profound and sweeping that he must handle them in
many various ways. Sometimes he translates the account of religious observances just as it is given in the
original. Sometimes he makes it Christian. And sometimes he mingles Christian and pagan in a single sentence.

[1] p. 313 D.   [2] p. 750 G.   [3] XXI 43, 15.
[4] p. 418 G.   [5] p. 458 L.   [6] p. 93 B.
[7] p. 445 D.

In the first place come those instances where Holland simply explains the names of the gods. "Juppiter optimus maximus" [1] is written "Jupiter Opt. Max. i. the best and greatest of all the gods." [2] He is also described as "that most bountifull and almighty god," [3] "that great good god," [4] or, with a direct adoption of Christian phrase, as "almightie and most gracious Jupiter." [5] On the other hand, when the translator feels that the meaning has been made sufficiently clear, no explanatory phrase is added. The proceeding is the same with the names of the other deities. After "Magna Mater" is written in brackets "the great mother of the gods"; [6] and after "Juventa," "the goddesse of youth." [7] "Lares" is translated "o yee Lares and domestical gods," [8] "penates" are usually called "the household gods." [9] "Patricia Pudicitia" appears as "Patritian Chastitie," [10] but again, in the same passage, as "Ladie Pudicitia Patritia." [10]

In general, the gods are left Roman when reference is made to their temples, particularly to the Capitol: "the Capitoll, the temple of Vesta, and other temples thereabout of the gods." [11] They are left Roman when any particular heathen customs are mentioned: he "called upon the gods, protectors of the law of hospitalitie"; [12]

[1] I 12, 7.
[2] p. 10 H.
[3] p. 99 C.
[4] p. 140 K.
[5] p. 698 M.
[6] p. 737 E.
[7] p. 429 A.
[8] p. 287 C.
[9] p. 214 L.
[10] p. 367 E.
[11] p. 200 I.
[12] p. 1056 I.

or "when upon a time he sacrificed unto the gods"; [1] or "Certain Oratours therefor were sent to the Oracle of Delphi, to know what the gods foresignified by that prodigious token." [2] Care is usually taken that they should be left Roman when the act described would be shameful to the Christian God: "Yet have some reverence, and stand in feare of the gods of your native countrey, which by your enemies are now taken prisoners and captivate." [3] Also when Romulus is called "dei filius," the phrasing must be changed: he obviously cannot be called "the son of God," but must be "the sonne of a god." [4]

On the other hand, pagan is made Christian whenever God is spoken of as a being to whom man turns for assistance and protection. "Now Gods helpe," [5] "a power of God hath assisted," [6] "defended by the speciall power and providence of God" [7] are some of the phrases that are used when the Latin word is variously "dei," "numen," "divinus," "religio." Also when it is a question of the divine being's willingness to bless mankind, there is a similar transformation to the Christian God: "the will and counsell of God should be sought for"; [8] and brief prayers become "God send us good lucke," [9]

---

[1] p. 899 C. [2] p. 190 G.
[3] p. 99 C. [4] p. 196 I.
[5] p. 211 C ("iam deorum opes," V 49, 5).
[6] p. 212 K ("numen . . . adfuit," V 51, 4).
[7] p. 85 E ("velut numine aliquo defensa castra," II 62, 2).
[8] p. 13 F.
[9] p. 1110 M ("si dis placet," XLI 23, 7).

or "God forbid and forfend." [1] Similarly when awesome or majestic qualities are suggested, "prodigious and strange tokens from heaven" threaten "the heavie hand of God." [2] And in time of trouble it becomes imperative for the people "to search forth the cause of Gods wrath and indignation," [3] although in the following sentences we learn that they sought it by inspecting "the inwards of sacrificed beasts, as by aspect of birds and foules."

Furthermore, the pagan Weltanschauung is frequently transformed into the Christian: "C. Julius the Censor departed this life." [4] Roman citizens who had no belief in a better world after death are made to speak of "the course of this world," [5] and "having but a while in this world to live." [6] The Devil is introduced: "eandem pestem ac furiam" [7] becomes "the same pestiferous furie, that fiend of hell, and limme of the devill." [8] "Quae malum" [9] is "in the devils name"; [10] and enemies killed in combat, instead of departing to the shades of the underworld, are "sent to the divell." [11] In addition to the change of specific pagan customs to their Christian equivalents, many Christian phrases are used where

---

[1] p. 318 K ("di meliora," IX 9, 6). Holland introduces several other Christian formulas of this sort. "Utinam" becomes "God grant," p. 168 M, or "Would to God," p. 226 L. "Bene vertat" is "God blesse us all," p. 130 K, or "Well, God speed our hand," p. 874 G. "Felices" is "a Gods name in happie houre," p. 78 G.

[2] p. 72 K.   [3] p. 72 L.   [4] p. 200 M.
[5] p. 213 A ("in rebus humanis," V 52, 1).
[6] p. 165 ("brevi reliquo vitae spatio," IV 41, 12).
[7] XXX 13, 13.   [8] p. 749 A.   [9] V 54, 6.
[10] p. 215 B.   [11] p. 18 L.

the Latin contained no reference to religion, but simply
a general statement of the courses of nature. "Sixe sons
God hath sent betweene us" [1] is the translation of "Sex
filii nobis . . . sunt." [2] "Nescio quo fato" [3] is expanded
into "How the divine providence of God hath appointed
it, I know not"; [4] "Uxorem sibi fato ereptam" [5] into
"I have buried my wife before, who died on Gods
hand." [6] Sometimes there is a simile from Christian
usage: "With an hideous and dissonant kind of singing
(*like a blacke Santus*) they filled all about with a fearefull and horrible noise." [7] Short Christian formulas
which have no parallel in the original appear at every
turn. These carry no particular thought of religion but
are calculated to add emphasis and reality to the speech.
Such are: "Go on in the name of God" [8] for "Agite
dum"; [9] or, when mention is made of the Greeks before
Troy, "How farre (good god) from their owne home?" [10]

But most striking of all are the occasions when Christian and pagan are blended in a single sentence with no
apparent consciousness on the translator's part of incongruity or contradiction. This assimilation of the
past in terms of the present is one of the most fascinat-
ing phases of the Renaissance. We have already ob-

---

[1] p. 1134 L.   [2] XLII 34, 4.   [3] III 19, 12.
[4] p. 101 E.   [5] III 50, 8.   [6] p. 121 C.
[7] p. 204 H (" truci cantu clamoribusque variis," V 37, 8).
[8] p. 130 K.   [9] III 62, 4.
[10] p. 182 G ("quam procul ab domo," V 4, 11). Other phrases put to a
similar use are "good Lord," "in the name of God," "for the love of God,"
"God forbid," "God wot," "so God me helpe."

served it in North. The same tendency accounted for the decoration of the choir in Chartres Cathedral with medallions representing Caesar and Hector. This attribution by a people of elements from their own religious system to that of a former system is a constant phenomenon in social change. It is similarly illustrated by the fifth century Ravenna mosaic of Christ in the garb of a Roman soldier.

Holland writes how there was assigned "unto Queene Juno a church." [1] He speaks of "a vestall Nun," [2] or again explains the Roman office by a Christian parallel: "He instituted also a Nunnerie as it were, of religious vestall virgines." [3] The desire to explain the function of the Roman office is perhaps responsible for such coupling as: "the Archbishop or High priest," [4] and "Sacrificers and Chaplaines." [5] But this cannot account for the blending in such sentences as "The gods said Amen and were on their side," [6] "A citie we have founded and built, by the will of God and due observation of Augurie and Auspice," [7] and "the Senate now destitute of all helpe and comfort of man, moved the people to devotion, to their beads, and praiers unto the gods." [8] For

---

[1] p. 195 D.   [2] p. 4 L.   [3] p. 14 M.

[4] p. 124 H ("pontifex maximus," III 54, 5).

[5] p. 339 C ("antistibus," IX 34, 18).

[6] p. 419 B ("diis auctoribus . . . acceptis," XXI 46, 2).

[7] p. 213 A ("Urben auspicato inauguratoque conditam habemus," V 52, 2).

[8] p. 92 L ("Inopsque senatus auxilii humani ad deos populum ac vota vertit," III 7, 7).

here the pagan elements have been so fully assimilated that their use has become unconscious.

What Holland did to make Livy an English classic may be finally and somewhat differently illustrated by an analysis of the way in which he handled the many speeches. From his point of view these could be put to very practical use: they could serve to instruct Englishmen in the art of oratory. So he placed at the end of his translation "A Table of all the Orations . . . fitted for all sorts of speaking or writing," [1] and divided them under many different heads including Persuasion, Dissuasion, Exhortation, Dehortation, Admonition, Petition, Praise, Prayer, Thanksgiving, Invective, Complaint, and Humble Entreaty. But he seems also to have perceived what has been objected by later critics, that Livy's speeches are too academic, that they have the dryness of a scholar in his study, not the natural animated cadences of the market place. From study to market place Holland proposed to take them. He did so by substituting direct discourse for many of Livy's passages of indirect discourse, especially when the content was an expression of a resolve, or an outpouring of joy or anger.[2] The result is extraordinarily effective:

[1] p. 1404 ff.
[2] Holland performs this with great variety and skill. Indirect discourse is left indirect when the speech is not important; when the words are the answer not of an individual but of a group; when an ambassador carries the words of his master; and in the early portions of the book, to fit the undeveloped speeches of the men of a crude society. Frequently Livy began a speech in direct discourse and then changed to indirect. Holland gives it

Hannibali nimis laeta res est visa maiorque, quam ut eam statim capere animo posset. Itaque voluntatem se laudare Maharabilis ait; ad consilium pensandum temporis opus esse. — XXII 51, 3.

No saith Anniball again, let curriers on Gods name go afore, and spare not to cary newes thereof: Your words are good, and it is a gay matter and plausible you speake of: but the way thereto is longer, and more than I can presently conceive and comprehend: I con you thanke, Maharaball, and I commend your good mind and forwardnesse; but we had need to deliberat and pause further upon this poynt. — p. 463 F–464 G.

But not only the use of direct discourse accounts for the fresh naturalness of such a speech. Holland develops all the tricks of the orator's art. He has a way of turning Livy's statements into rhetorical questions. "But he ... *what did he else but disarme you, and as it were,* take your weapons from you, and offer you naked to *the devotion and mercie of* your bondmen and outlawes?"[1] is what he gives for "Hic ... arma vobis ademit nudosque servis vestris et exsulibus obiecit."[2]   He also inserts short phrases, "And why?", "For why?", to point contrasts: Terentillus inveighed against the regiment of the Consuls thus: "For in name only (*quoth he*) lesse odious *and hatefull* it is than that of the KK [Kings], but *in fact* in very deed, *more grievous and* cruell. *For why?* In steed of one lord, *the cittie* hath received twaine."[3]

greater naturalness by making it wholly direct. On the other hand, the translator sometimes sets off an important sentence or two in a long passage of indirect discourse by turning it into direct.

[1] p. 101 B–C.   [2] III 19, 6.   [3] p. 93 E.

Other phrases are added to suggest the actual swing of speech: "No commoner (*ye might be sure*) would have forced a daughter of any noble house," [1] "*consider*, I beseech you, *and see:* the love and pleasure of hunting carrieth men," [2] "*And now behold (quoth he) by the onelie goodnesse of M. Manlius, I have the libertie againe* to see the light *of the sunne*." [3] The expansion of this last from "videre lucem . . . M. Manli opera" [4] also reveals how greater scope is given to the speaker's emotions.

A full rhetorical pomp comes naturally to Holland's pen. He knows that an orator must assume elaborate robes. Consequently, in the speech of Appius Claudius against the Tribunes, he doubles with rare skill both word and phrase: "Now let them mocke on *and scoffe* at our religions. *Let them deride our ceremonies.* What makes matter (*say they*) if those pullets *pecke or* eat not? What if they come *somewhat* late out of their coupe *or cage?* What if a bird sing *auke or crowe crosse and* contrarie? *How then? A great piece of matter surely.* Small things but, *I confesse*, they be: but as small as they are, our auncestours by not contemning them, have brought this C.[ommon] W.[ealth] to a flourishing state." [5]

---

[1] p. 142 K. These expressions include: "behold," "lo," "looke," "see," "I pray you," "I assure you," "I beseech you."

[2] p. 183 B. [3] p. 226 G.

[4] VI 14, 8.

[5] p. 247 C–D. ("Eludant nunc licet religiones, 'quid enim esse, si pulli non pascantur, si ex cavea tardius exierint, si occecinerit avis?' Parva sunt haec; sed parva ista non contemnendo maiores nostri maximam hanc rem fecerunt," VI 41, 8–9).

The translator throws himself wholly into the spirit of the forum. He seems to feel himself actually standing before the Roman Senate, and where Livy always addressed this body by the official "patres conscripti," Holland varies his words according to the speaker. A senator faces his associates with "My lords." [1] A foreign ambassador begins the account of his mission with "Most noble Senatours." [2] And when captives plead for redemption, they say "Right honourable, and my very good L.L. [Lords] of the Senate." [3] On occasion Holland becomes so immersed in the character of the speaker that he adds whole sentences in the middle of his address: "But will you have the truth?" or "But be you not dismaied." Then it is that he pens the orations that he hopes will be most useful to his countrymen in "all sorts of speaking and writing":

Sine, timidum pro cauto, tardum pro considerato, imbellum pro perito belli vocent. Malo, te sapiens hostis metuat, quam stulti cives laudent. Omnia audentem contemnet Hannibal, nihil temere agentem metuet. — XXII 39, 20.

Let them call you *and spare not*, fearefull for carefull, *cold and* slow for *wise and* considerate, an ill souldiour *and ignorant* for a skilful warrior *and experienced. But be not you dismaied:* I had liefer *heare* a wise *and sober* enemie to fear you, than see foolish *and braine-sicke* cittizens to praise you. *Adventure* all things boldly, Anniball will contemne you: enterprise nothing rashly, he shall dread you. — p. 457 B.

p. 469 E.　　　　　[2] p. 269 A.　　　　　[3] p. 468 I.

V

A study of the translator general ought not to be based on a single book. To establish and enlarge the impression given by Holland's *Livy* it is well to turn to his *Suetonius*. For the two originals were works of very different scope. The *History of Twelve Caesars* was saved from being a book of scandal by the earnestness of its author's purpose and his passion for facts. If a love of the curious and abnormal caused him to strip away the robe of glory from even Julius Caesar and Augustus, his aim was to reveal their virtues and vices alike, to portray them not as emperors but as men. Such an aim recommended him highly to Holland and his contemporaries, since they took great delight in his genius for the details of biography. A like genius for the trivial and intimate gained expression in their own books of anecdotes, in the pictures which Wood and Aubrey were destined to give of Holland himself.

The translator admired Suetonius for his "uncorrupt and plaine truth," [1] for having penned the lives of the emperors with the same liberty as they had lived. And "if happlie in prosecuting of this point, he hath recorded ought that may be offensive to chast and modest mindes," Holland's recommendation is that "yee shal do well to glaunce over with your eye such places lightly,

---

[1] Holland, *Suetonius*, Tudor Translations, ed. C. Whibley (London, 1899) I, 3. All page references are to this edition.

as I with my pen touched unwillingly." [1] No thought of the brutality of the book prevented him from dedicating it to Lady Harington, or declaring that his purpose in translating it was to "benefit young Scholars." He handles Suetonius very much like Livy. Exactly the same things happen to the Latin: when Caesar, crossing the Rubicon, says, "Iacta alea est," [2] it becomes in Holland: "The die be throwne. I have set up my rest. Come what will of it." [3] It is unnecessary to record once more the qualities of his style, since they are quickly seen to be identical in all his work. Livy, Plutarch, and Suetonius all walk through London streets in the same garb. But certain elements in the *Suetonius* throw into greater relief some of Holland's powers.

He perceives that the most essential quality in Suetonius is the closeness and familiarity of his details, and he devotes himself to these with the same care that he gave to Livy's speeches. Sometimes he brings them home to his reader by the rhetorical fullness of his style, as when he relates how Nero "pronounced even with *expresse* gesture *like a player*, certaine ridiculous rimes, and those set to lascivious *and wanton* measures, against

[1] I, 3.

[2] Suetonius, *De Vita Caesarum*, Book I, chap. 32. All references are to the Loeb Library edition with a translation by J. C. Rolfe (New York, 1914). Mr. Rolfe states in his preface: "The version of Philemon Holland . . . cannot be surpassed in style and spirit, and it is more accurate than any other English translation. An attempt has been made to compete with it in the only possible way, namely in greater fidelity to a better text than was available in his day, and in a nearer approach to the manner of Suetonius."

[3] I, 39.

the chiefetaines of rebellion: *and what were those? even
stale stuffe* and commonly known already." [1] But it is
soon apparent that Holland himself possesses an extraordinary eye for detail. In the description of Nero's
appearance he speaks of "the tender downe of his beard
new budding forth," [2] which the Latin had simply
called "lanuginem eius." [3] He also mentions his "fine
Lawne neck Kercheif," [4] which Suetonius had termed
"sudario." [5] Thus is the translator true not to the
letter, but to the spirit of the original.

There is an extraordinary magic in this added detail.
It gives new richness to the context to translate "insignes pinguissima coma et excellentissimo cultu" [6]
(which the modern version renders "These men were
noticeable for their thick hair and fine apparel") by the
fully relished "deft and trim boyes, such as had the
thickest bush of haire upon their heads, and were set out
in most excellent apparell." [7] A vividness clings to the
statement, "Hee exacted also with great skornefulnesse
and extremitie, *good* money rough *and new coyned,* silver
fine and full of risings: golde *pure and* red *as fire*" [8] which
is unknown to the compact "nummum asperum, argen-
tum pustulatum, aurum ad obrussam." [9] And when it is
said of Augustus that "after supper hee retired himselfe

[1] II, 141 ("Iocularia in defectionis duces carmina lasciveque modulata,
quae vulgo notuerunt, etiam gesticulatus est," VI 42, 2).

[2] II, 131.   [3] VI 34, 5.   [4] II, 150.
[5] VI 51.   [6] VI 20, 3.   [7] II, 114.
[8] II, 142–143. [9] VI 44, 2.

into a little Closet or Studie. And there continued hee
by a candle farre in the night," [1] the addition of the words
"by a candle" raises the whole scene before our eyes.

Holland shows abundant power in bringing new colors
and odors into his pages. In the account of a magnificent banquet, "rosaria" [2] is translated as "rose water
and odoriferous oyles or perfumes of Roses from Syr-
tium." [3] It is "the yvorie curule chaire," [4] "two cuppes
of Chrystall," [5] "a fine yellow veile," [3] where none of the
substances were specified by Suetonius. Many of Holland's enlargements were not suggested by anything in
the original, but greater animation nearly always results
from them. It certainly does so when the "aretelagos" [6]
or story-tellers which Augustus introduced at his feasts
are described as "these discoursing poore threedbare
Phylosophers." [7]

Holland also heightens the pitch by some of the dramatic methods we observed in Florio. "*Well*, the world
having indured such an Emperour *as this*, little lesse
than 14 yeares, at length *fell away and* forsooke him
cleane" [8] has a narrative swing not felt in the Latin. A
story-teller rather than an historian translates this book.
He has the gift of making a contrast stronger. To suggest Domitius' full shame in requiring ladies and gentle-

---

[1] I, 146 (". . . ad multam noctem permanebat," II 78).

[2] VI 27, 3.   [3] II, 122.   [4] II, 109.

[5] II, 145.   [6] II, 74.   [7] I, 144.

[8] II, 138. ("Talem principem paulo minus quattuordecim annos per-
pessus terrarum orbis tandem destituit," VI 40, 1).

men of noble rank to appear on the stage, it is stated that he had them "acte a *Comicall and wanton* Enterlude."[1] Further than this, there is an actual adoption of the dramatist's or novelist's art. When the provinces are in danger Nero chatters on about his trifles: "That unskilfulnesse, *forsooth*, was objected unto him in that very art, which he had so painfully studied and brought to so good perfection: and therewith asked them *eftsones* one by one, whether they had ever knowen a more excellent Musician than himselfe."[2] There is nothing in the tone of "forsooth" or "eftsones" in the original, and the way in which Holland uses them does much to suggest the affectation of Nero's voice. A few pages later the end has come. Nero, finally aroused to terror, has fled from Rome by night, and is overtaken by a messenger with official letters. "And reading therein that hee had his Dome by the Senate, To be an Enemie *to the State*: That he *was laid for all about* to be punished, More maiorum. '*More maiorum!*' *quoth he*, 'what kinde of punishment is that?'"[3] The original runs, "Legitque se hostem a senatu iudicatum et quaeri, ut puniatur more maiorum, interrogavitque quale id genus esset poenae."[4] Great intensity is added by the change to direct speech, and there is something keenly pitiful in the repetition of the fatal words "More maiorum" when it is known "that the man so condemned should be script

---

[1] II, 101 ("ad agendum mimum," VI 4).
[2] II, 140.   [3] II, 148.   [4] VI 49, 2.

all naked, his head locked fast in a forke, and his body scourged with rods to death." [1]

Another thing that is perhaps even more noticeable in the *Suetonius* than in the *Livy* is the way the book seems to have been made in England. Its scenes do not reveal ancient Rome but contemporary London. When a royal procession goes "all about the shire-townes of great resort and market burroughes of Greece," [2] we think of Kent or Warwickshire. We are in the same London as that revealed by the dramatists when we hear that Augustus enjoyed watching not only the boxing champions, "but such also as out of the common sort of townes-men, fell together by the eares pell mell in the narrow streets"; [3] or when we read, as a rendering for "sordidos ac deparcos," [4] not "stingy and niggardly fellows," but "base niggards and mechanicall pinch-pennies"; [5] or when an emperor's "asturconem" [6] is "his ambling guelding"; [7] or when, in a celebration, "birdes were let fly, ribbands also and labels yea and sweete banketting junkets cast along." [8]

The speech of Englishmen appears on every page, that robust slang which false politeness was soon destined to bar from written prose. They are not emperors

---

[1] II, 148.

[2] II, 122 ("circa conventus mercatusque Graeciae," VI 28, 2).

[3] I, 122 ("sed et catevarios oppidanos inter angustias vicorum pugnantis," II 45, 2).

[4] VI 30, 1.   [5] II, 123.

[6] VI 46, 1.   [7] II, 144.

[8] II, 120 ("ingestaeque aves ac lemnisci et bellaria," VI 25, 2).

but men whom Holland is talking about. "Claudius
went for a foole, and one of the laughing stocks of the
Court." [1] Nero would break into song "if he had sippled
a little and wet his whistle." [2] And the last shred of vain
majesty is torn away from this monstrous weakling
when he is described with "his belly and paunch bearing
out: with a paire of passing slender spindle shanks." [3]
Such fine slang is the very substance of Holland's style.
The direct statement "But when some gave evasive an-
swers and some openly refused" [4] becomes "But when
some of them made it coy and kept some hafting: others
in plaine termes refused." [5] Edicts of Vindex are described as "comming so thicke one in the necke of another." [6] "Nevertheless he did not abandon" [7] is what
the twentieth century has substituted for "Neither yet
for all this strucke he saile one whit." [8]

To be sure such language sometimes lacks subtlety
and is overstrong, as for instance, in the fantastic sentence: "M. Antonius hitteth him in the teeth with his
great Grandfather: saying he was but a Libertine
borne." [9] But page by page it possesses the greatest
quality that a translation can achieve: the inevitability
of prose perfectly naturalized. You forget that you are

[1] II, 103 ("Claudius inter ludibria aulae erat," VI 6, 2).
[2] II, 113 ("si paulum subbibisset," VI 20, 2).
[3] II, 150 ("ventre proiecto, gracillimis cruribus," VI, 51).
[4] Rolfe's version of VI 47, 2.
[5] II, 145.   [6] II, 139.
[7] Rolfe's version of VI 42, 2.   [8] II, 141.
[9] I, 82 ("M. Antonius libertinum ei proavum exprobrat," II 2, 3).

not reading an original when you come to this detail about Augustus: "In steede of drinke hee tooke a sop of bread soaked in colde water; or a peece of Coucumber, or a young letuce head, or else some new gathered apple, sharpe and tart, standing much upon a winish liquour within it." [1] Yet it follows the Latin practically word for word.

At times unnecessary fullness detracts from the compact strength of Suetonius, as in the account of the burial of Britannicus. "But the next morrow, in all hast hee tooke order for his corps to bee caried forth to buriall, with no better funerals than ordinarie; and that, in an exceeding great storme of raine" [2] is substituted for the piercing "Postero die raptim inter maximos imbres tralaticio extulit funere." [3] But such diffuseness is not frequent, and generally does not touch the extraordinarily powerful descriptions. Take as a last example this picture of the great Augustus, where the art of Suetonius has lost nothing under Holland's pen and the English as well as the Latin is a masterpiece:

Hee had a paire of cleere and shining eyes: wherein also, (as hee would have made men beleeve) was seated a kinde of Divine vigour: and hee joyed much, if a man looking wistly upon him helde downe his face, as it were against the brightnesse of the Sunne. But in his olde age he saw not very well with the left eye. His teeth grewe thinne in his head, and the

[1] I, 146 ("Pro potione sumebat perfusum aqua frigida panem aut cucumeris frustum vel lactuculae thyrsum aut recens aridumve pomum suci vinosioris," II, 77).

[2] II, 128.   [3] VI 33, 3.

same were small and ragged: the haire of his head was somewhat curled and turning downeward; and withall of a light
yellowe colour. His eye-browes met together: his eares were
of a meane bignesse: his nose both in the upper part, bearing
out round, and also beneath somewhat with the longest.[1]

His stature was short, but "his shoes underlaide somewhat with the highest, that he might seeme taller than
he was." [2]

The translator completed his work with a set of annotations which are learned, if not always wholly relevant.
They also fulfill his purpose of bringing the book home
to his readers. He explains a reference to Caesar's cos-
tume by saying: "In steede of our Breeches and Stock-
ings, the Greeks and Romans used in those daies certaine loose cloathes in manner of Swathling bands to
cover and lap their nakednesse." [3] He writes a vigorous
note on "Sumptuaria": "Many lawes went under the
title Sumptuaria, to represse the immoderate expense in
apparell, and belly-cheere especially." [4] He states that
the English equivalent of "Festina lente" is "The soft
fire makes sweet malt." [5] He shows throughout the same
passionate enthusiasm for knowledge that vivified his
prefaces, and enabled him to write at the close of his
Livy:

I doubt not but many of them who shall take delight and
pleasure in reading the Romane storie above written, will
presently grow into a liking of the very place, which hath

[1] I, 147–148 (II 79, 2).   [2] I, 144 (II 73).
[3] I, 266.   [4] I, 255.   [5] I, 253.

affourded so woorthy persons and rare examples. The love whereof hath moved many a man to undertake a voiage to Rome, onely to see the river Tyberis, those seven hils, and the monuments remaining of that famous citie. The journie they have found, for way long and tedious; for expense of money heavie and chargeable; for hazard of religion, conscience and good manners, exceeding dangerous: so farre degenerate are the inhabitants now from that auncient people, so devoute, so vertuous and uncorrupt, in old time. To satisfie the readers in this behalfe, and to avoid the perill of that travaile, I thought it not amisse to bring Rome (as it were) home to them, even to represent unto their eye the topographie thereof.[1]

Thus he saved his readers a trip to Rome by fifty-six folio pages of description of her ancient monuments.[2] He compiled them with a relish, since it seemed to him that he was bringing his countrymen something as rich and fertile as the impressions gained in travel. The most important fact in accounting for the freshness of both the poetry and prose of the early seventeenth century is that the men of that day possessed what Mr. T. S. Eliot has so accurately called "the direct sensuous apprehension of thought." [3] Because Holland's thoughts came to him with the same immediacy as the odor of a rose, he could conceive of his vast labor of translation as a long journey abroad:

---

[1] *Livy*, 1346.

[2] "A Summarie Collected by Iohn Bartholomew Marlianus, a Gentleman of Millane, Touching the Topographie of Rome in Ancient Time."

[3] *Homage to John Dryden*, Three Essays on Poetry of the Seventeenth Century (London, 1924), p. 29.

I for my part, having struggled with the difficulties of the Alpes & in some sort overcome them; crossed Rhosne and the Po; passed over the hils Olympus and Aemus, & scrawled through the rough streights of Thermopylae and Tempe, seeme now I would not in my returne to stick at the pleasant mounts, Palatine, Capitol, Aventin, & with the plains and vallies between, or the river Tybre & Mars field underneath them, beautified especially with such stately temples, triumphant arches, glorious pallaces, Theatres, Cirques, Columnes, & Colosses; wonders of the world.[1]

And because he could so conceive his task, a translation from his hands is not a piece of lifeless hack work, but a magnificent stirring masterpiece of prose.

[1] *Livy*, 1346.

CHAPTER VI

Conclusion

NATURALLY the general qualities of the Elizabethan translator are revealed in varying proportions in the work of the four men treated here. One reason why these men serve so excellently as a full illustration of their art is that among them they embrace so many important tendencies. Hoby, for example, in both his point of view and capabilities, marks the period just before the full Renaissance. A disciple of Cheke, his theory of strictly accurate translation is in accord with the ideals of the early humanists; and, in order to suggest the relation of his work to its background, I outlined in brief their general position. His translation is of absorbing interest because it reveals in embryo the qualities that were to characterize the later full Elizabethan speech. Although he follows the Italian very closely, his Courtier is wholly an Englishman. A comparison of Hoby's robust, frequently stumbling prose with the polished, easy periods of Castiglione gives in essence the whole difference between English and Italian society in the first half of the sixteenth century.

Florio, on the other hand, is as symbolical of the close of Elizabeth's reign as Hoby is of the beginning. Instructor in Italian to the ladies and gentlemen of the court, he was so much the fastidious pedant that romancing critics have taken him for the original of Shakespeare's Holofernes in *Love's Labour's Lost*. His translation of Montaigne is not free from extravagance and affectation; its words reflect the fashions of the day, the vogue of Lyly and Du Bartas. But they catch also the splendid energy of the dramatists, and although they are sometimes at a distance from the original, they enmesh more of Montaigne's sixteenth-century spirit than any later version, and they brought him into a form that fired the imagination of Shakespeare.

The influence of North's words upon Shakespeare was even more profound. For North was a far greater craftsman than Florio. His translation indicates the channel by which a large part of the new learning came to England: he did not translate from the Greek of Plutarch, but from the intermediary French of Jacques Amyot. This does not mean that his book is not close to the original, for Amyot was a great scholar who had done his work faithfully. On the other hand, in far more subtle ways than Florio was capable of, North re-made Plutarch in the image of an Englishman. Examine his prose and you will find that it follows Amyot, cadence for cadence, and almost word for word. And yet each book reflects its translator: Amyot was a scholar and a bishop, North was a country gentleman and captain of three hundred men against the Armada. Among the translators of the period he was perhaps the greatest artist. For in almost impalpable ways his personality became fused with his work.

Philemon Holland was one of the few scholars in this Elizabethan craft. Sir Thomas Hoby was Elizabeth's ambassador to the court of France. Florio's greatest boast was his appointment as gentleman-extraordinary and groom of the Privy Chamber under James I. Neither of them possessed the first requisite of a modern translator: a thorough knowledge of the language of the original. They made some ludicrous mistakes. But in compensation they had what has fallen to the lot of few of their successors: a fertile and varied command of their own tongue. Holland, however, was capable both of rare labors with Greek and Latin folios, and of an equally rare prose style. His scholarship is outranked by that of Henry Savile, who translated Tacitus, but no one can threaten his position of translator general to his age. Livy, Pliny, Plutarch's *Morals*, Suetonius, Ammianus Marcellinus, and Xenephon all yielded to the valor of his pen. In his work is revealed more fully than anywhere else the process through which an ancient classic became modern. His purpose was always double: to make the book easy for his reader, and to bring out its important qualities to the full. He achieved this with so great mastery that his prose possesses the inevitability of an original. His descriptions of the Roman emperors are as closely intimate as those of an eyewitness. Under his hand, as under those of the rest, translation became a great art. And the reason is that the past was not looked upon as something dead. Livy and Suetonius were as alive to Holland's imagination as were any of his contemporaries of flesh and blood. In this belief he presented them to his monarch, confident that they would be of great service to the whole realm.

The average translation does not last long. It is either a useful crib with no style of its own, and simply a pale reflection of the original; or the style of the translator's generation intrudes upon it and makes it lively for the time being, but generally unsatisfactory after twenty years. The translator must either suppress his personality and produce a scholarly work, faultless, but without life; or, if he enters creatively into his work, he runs the almost certain risk of adding elements which the next generation will consider a clouding of the spirit of the original. The Elizabethan translators all sinned in this second way, and yet their work has endured as a part of English literature as no other group of translations has. Sometimes they were saved by being closer to the temper of the original than any later writer could hope to be. In spite of all his limitations, Florio's contemporaneity with Montaigne gave his translation more of the tang of the *Essays* than has filtered into the pages of any other version; just as, for similar reasons, Constance Garnett's *Dostoevsky* will probably remain the standard, and Scott Moncrieff's *Proust*. But the great miracles of

North's *Plutarch* and the Bible can be explained only by the fortunate circumstances of the Elizabethan age. Knowledge was fresh, language could be bent to one's will, thoughts swarmed so eagerly that they could not be separated from emotions. The language was more fully alive than it has ever been, which means that the people were also.

Date Due